Praise for *Content to Commerce*

"Social media has fundamentally changed the way we do business today. This book is a terrific blueprint for how brands can successfully drive social media marketing at scale."

—**Pete Cashmore,** CEO and founder, Mashable

"Avi Savar was a savant when it came to knowing that brands were becoming the new media long before most had any idea this was the case, Now with *Content to Commerce*, he illuminates the path from theory to operational practice—convincingly showing that, to indeed be the new media, brands have to act much like a traditional broadcasting network."

—**Marisa Thalberg,** VP, Corporate Global Digital Marketing,
The Estée Lauder Companies, Inc.

"In the quickly changing, enigmatic world of digital marketing, it is critical for us to learn how to navigate across paid, earned, and owned media channels. Avi Savar has helped many marketers evolve from staid models of talking at consumers to truly engaging them with their brands. Anyone who wants to advance their skills in the fascinating world of digital content and social media will benefit from this book."

—**Mindel Klein Lepore,** Marketing Director,
Integrated Marketing Communications,
Colgate-Palmolive Company

"Years of experience, trial, error, and insight condensed into a comprehensive road map to successful social media marketing."

—**Bill Davenport,** Executive Producer, Wieden+Kennedy

"Social media is constantly evolving, and brands need to keep up with the movement to engage with consumers the right way. This book will help you understand the importance of social media and how it has direct impact on your business beyond a like or a tweet."

—**Peter DeLuca,** SVP, Brand & Advertising, T-Mobile USA

"Today in the age of the people's network, social marketing has become critical. Avi Savar has been a leader in the social space but goes beyond ordinary thinking to practice at the intersection of content, commerce and network effects. How can you leverage paid, owned, and earned marketing in an age when transactions can be measured and content is increasingly key? *Content to Commerce* illuminates the way ahead!"

—**Rishad Tobaccowala,** Chief Strategy and
Innovation Officer, VivaKi

"As a digital marketer you begin to realize that conversations are going on with or without your brand's participation. Learn easy and effective ways to join the discussion, letting your voice be heard through Savar's easy-to-follow approach."

—**Leslie C. Reiser,** Director, Digital Marketing, IBM

"Avi Savar has been seeing around corners in media and marketing for as long as I've known him, only this time he is inviting readers along for the ride. Strap on!"

—**Richard Siklos,** Vice President, Time Warner, Inc.

"Social media has become today's word-of-mouth marketing, with a powerful twist. Great brands can engage customers and leverage technology beyond mere likes and chatter. Avi Savar has a unique perspective on creating content and incorporating the right tools that not only drive conversation but lead to meaningful business results."

—**Lee Nadler,** Marketing Communications Manager,
MINI USA

"Avi Savar offers crucial insight into social media to a wide and thoughtful readership. Part textbook, part operating system, thoroughly entertaining, it functions like a platform for practitioners in social media to build upon its wisdom and learnings for years to come."

—**Dean Baker,** Managing Director,
JWT Entertainment

"If you're interested in mastering the 'art of social,' this is the book for you. There are very few masters in this world, and it just so happens Avi is one of them, which makes all of us fortunate that he took the time to put his brain on paper. You know what they say about when fortune strikes . . . "

—**Dave Balter,** CEO, BzzAgent

"Read this book fast. *Content to Commerce: Engaging Consumers Across Paid, Owned, and Earned Channels* doesn't just illuminate where digital marketing has been and where it's going; it promises to help you get there before everyone else beats you to it."

—**Ross Martin,** Executive Vice President,
MTV Scratch

"Avi Savar is a world-class expert leading this exciting and ever-changing part of the communications landscape."

—**Philip Thomas,** Chief Executive Officer,
Cannes Lions International
Festival of Creativity

"Building brands on social media is more important today then ever before. Avi breaks down the secret into an easy to follow guide for marketing success."

—**Michael Scissons,** Founder and
CEO, Syncapse

"At a time when brands talk of being publishers, Content to Commerce shows you how to create the type of content that people really want and that will have other brands asking their agencies to 'get me one of those.'

—**Nick Friese,** CEO, Digiday

"Avi's 'NEW model' is quickly becoming THE model!"

—**Jon Bond,** former advertising wizard and founder,
Kirshenbaum Bond and Partners

"Our consumers are evolving; the paradigm has shifted from pure exposure to intrinsic engagement. New messaging strategies are needed to engage your advocates across multiple touch points. Avi Savar delivers the perfect book at the perfect time. Be inspired!"

—**Silvia Goh,** Chief Content Officer,
LiquidThread China,
Starcom MediaVest Group

"Avi Savar makes the clear case for why mastering content marketing isn't a cool check-the-box tactic but a business imperative for brands (and brand executives) that hope to remain relevant in the social age."

—**Scott Donaton,** CEO, Ensemble Branded
Entertainment; author of *Madison &
Vine: Why the Entertainment and
Advertising Industries Must
Converge to Survive*

"There used to be a wall, with content on one side and commerce on the other. But as Avi Savar so keenly explains, that wall is tumbling down. His experience bridges the worlds of content and brands—and in these valuable pages he shares what he has learned and where we're going. If you're a brand manager, content creator, or web curator, you'll want to dig into these pages with gusto!"

—**Steve Rosenbaum,** CEO, Magnify.net, and Entrepreneur at Large, NYCEDC

"Whether you are a social media newcomer, an established social expert, or the chief digital officer of a large brand advertiser or digital agency, Avi's book has a plethora of tips, tactics, and stories on how to think about social media and establish new social media paradigms within your organization."

—**Alan Osetek,** Global President, Resolution Media, an Omnicom Media Group Company

"Ignore Avi Savar at your peril. Intensely creative, yet focused and practical, he creates a virtual how-to guide to a new way of marketing that he virtually invented. . . . and keeps reinventing."

—**Bob Meyers,** President and COO, TRA, Inc.

"Until I read this book by Avi Savar, I thought I knew something about the role of content in social networks. I was blind and now I can see"

—**Rodrigo Figueroa Reyes,** Founder and CEO, FiRe Advertainment

"If you want to understand how to incorporate content into your marketing messaging, this book is a must read. Avi is a rare blend—one part content producer, one part ad man. He gives you a blueprint for success!"

—**Jon Vlassopulos,** CEO, Trailerpop

"In *Content to Commerce*, Avi Savar goes future to present."

—**Marc Ros,** Founder and CEO, AFTERSHARE.TV

"Rename this book to *Taking It to the Bank* because that is what you will be doing, time and time again if you follow the advice in *Content to Commerce*!!"

—**Jeffrey Hayzlett,** best-selling author, global business celebrity, and sometimes cowboy

CONTENT

TO

ENGAGING CONSUMERS
ACROSS PAID,

COMMERCE

OWNED, AND
EARNED CHANNELS

AVI SAVAR

WILEY

Published by John Wiley & Sons, Inc., Hoboken, New Jersey.
Published simultaneously in Canada.

For general information about our other products and services, please contact our Customer Care Department within the United States at (800) 762–2974, outside the United States at (317) 572–3993 or fax (317) 572–4002.

Wiley publishes in a variety of print and electronic formats and by print-on-demand. Some material included with standard print versions of this book may not be included in e-books or in print-on-demand. If this book refers to media such as a CD or DVD that is not included in the version you purchased, you may download this material at http://booksupport.wiley.com. For more information about Wiley products, visit www.wiley.com.

Library of Congress Cataloging-in-Publication Data:
Savar, Avi, 1973–
    Content to commerce: engaging consumers across paid, owned and earned channels/Avi Savar.
      pages cm
    Includes bibliographical references and index.
    ISBN 978-1-118–48018-2 (cloth); ISBN 978-1-118–66061-4 (ebk); ISBN 978-1-118-52646-0 (ebk); ISBN 978-1-118-52629-3 (ebk)
  1. Social marketing.   2. Internet marketing.   I. Title.
    HF5414.S378 2013
    658.8'72—dc23   2013001304

Printed in the United States of America

10 9 8 7 6 5 4 3 2 1

To my wife and daughter, who inspire me every day.
Without them, nothing is possible.

CONTENTS

ABOUT THIS BOOK

Almost all books on the subject of social media are, at some point, about conversations. This book is, too—but unlike many others, it is also *based on* conversations. *Content to Commerce* presents a uniquely comprehensive approach to social marketing called the network model, and it does so with the help of more than 20 prominent thought leaders and practitioners.

The network model draws much of its inspiration from TV programming practices. Here again, the book does so as well. It weaves in excerpts from multiple interviews in the manner of the best TV documentaries, punctuating and elaborating on the content through third-party expertise and experiences. Chapters are populated with illuminating sidebars that highlight both insights of individual contributors and virtual conversations among various collaborators.

This book is structured so that it does not have to be read from cover to cover, although newcomers to social media marketing may choose to do so to help establish their credentials. Veterans will also find something of value in all chapters, which are organized into six sections.

Section I: Brand as Network

Chapter 1, "Beyond Publishing," expands on the conventional wisdom that marketers must "think like a publisher," contending that this concept has become too limited in light of the growing influence of social media across all facets of marketing and beyond.

Chapter 2, "Social Media Is an Octopus," explores the multiple social touch points that brands and their marketers must take into account when connecting with consumers.

Chapter 3, "Social Media Is a Complex System," picks up on Chapter 2 and examines how the ongoing interaction among such social touch points, platforms, and channels—plus paid, owned, and earned media—creates more and more complex challenges.

Chapter 4, "The Brand Network," introduces a new and more comprehensive way of thinking about social media marketing, one that elevates the notion of "brand as publisher" to "brand as network" and enables marketers to successfully handle the increasing breadth and complexity of social media.

Chapter 5, "Business Solutions," presents a set of proven and repeatable processes that can be used to achieve any type of social marketing strategy.

Section II: The Value of the Network

Chapter 6, "Higher Highs and Higher Lows," underscores one of the principal advantages of the network model: to amplify, build, and sustain optimal levels of long-term audience engagement throughout social marketing campaigns.

Chapter 7, "Amplification," specifically focuses on how brands can strategically use tent-pole events to reach high points of consumer awareness and keep up continued interest throughout a long campaign.

Chapter 8, "Continuity," demonstrates how to further advance audience engagement through effective channel and community management.

Chapter 9, "Operations," takes a look at the critical roles that technology and talent play in maintaining a well-oiled brand network.

Section III: Audience First

Chapter 10, "Building Bridges," reveals why brands must shift their perspective from focusing on their own products and services (commerce-based marketing) to addressing the needs and interests of consumers (content-based marketing).

Chapter 11, "Welcome to the Party," explains how best to achieve this new perspective by creating "people stories" that arouse audiences' interests rather than "product stories" that are essentially sales messages.

Chapter 12, "Mutual Priorities," shows how brands can match their priorities with those of current and potential customers.

Chapter 13, "Audience Insights," illustrates how to combine strategy and analytics into a single approach to listening and learning about what is important to targeted audiences.

Chapter 14, "The Art and Science of Listening," expands on Chapter 3 by focusing on the value of the engagement point: the sweet spot where a brand's objectives, consumers' interests, and their perceptions of a brand's products and services all come together to define the relationship between a brand and its audience.

Section IV: Content Is Currency

Chapter 15, "Content at the Speed of Culture," considers the various features of the "always-on" social ecosystem in which brands create content and audiences consume it.

Chapter 16, "Content That Connects," tells how to develop and produce engaging content across the expanding range of social channels and platforms.

Chapter 17, "The Creative Process," exhibits the two key elements of successful social campaigns: creating compelling content and making it as easy as possible for audiences to find it.

Chapter 18, "Taking Measure," highlights the three key measurement pillars in the network model: inspiration, distribution, and scorekeeping.

Section V: Looking Ahead

Chapter 19, "Looking Out," explores the role of social media in an increasingly global and mobile economy.

Chapter 20, "Looking In," peers beyond marketing to examine how brands may incorporate social throughout their organizations.

Epilogue

The book concludes with Chapter 21, "The Question," 13 brief essays from leading social media professionals, all answering the question, "If you were going to build a marketing organization from scratch today, how would you do it?"

CAST OF CHARACTERS

Through a series of interviews and conversation the following individuals have played key roles in the creation of *Content to Commerce*.

The Thought Leaders

Stephanie Agresta
Global Director of Social Media and Digital, MSLGROUP

As MSLGROUP's global director of social media and digital, Stephanie Agresta works in partnership with leaders of the global network on social and digital vision, strategy, and talent in support of the agency's global social media offering, Social Hive. In addition to launching "Bloggers Lounge," a networking hub for digital media influencers at the South by Southwest conference, she founded Stephanie Agresta Consulting, a digital marketing firm that forged partnerships with noted digital thought leaders and emerging technology companies. Agresta is a popular speaker at industry events and serves on the board of directors of the Social Media Advertising Consortium. In 2010, she was named to *PRWeek*'s "40 Under 40" roster, and in the same year, her first book, *Perspectives on Social Media Marketing*, was released.

Pete Blackshaw
Global Head of Digital Marketing and Social Media, Nestlé S.A.

Prior to his current position at Nestlé, Pete Blackshaw was chief marketing officer of NM Incite, a recent joint venture between Nielsen and McKinsey centering on enterprise social media strategy and insights. He recently authored the book *Satisfied Customers Tell Three Friends, Angry Customers Tell 3,000: Running a Business in Today's Consumer-Driven World*, and he writes a regular column in *Advertising Age* that focuses on the book's themes. Blackshaw founded PlanetFeedback.com, cofounded the Word-of-Mouth Marketing Association, served as chair of the board of the National Council of Better Business Bureaus, and is a member of the National Advertising Review Council. He is a 2010 grand prize winner of the "Great Minds" award from the Advertising Research Foundation.

Reggie Bradford
Senior Vice President of Product Development, Oracle Founder and Former Chief Executive Officer, Vitrue

Veteran technology and management executive Reggie Bradford is senior vice president of product development for Oracle, where he brings more than 20 years of experience across technology, Internet, and marketing sectors. Prior to joining Oracle, he was founder and chief executive officer of Vitrue (now a wholly owned subsidiary of Oracle), where he developed the company into the leading provider of social marketing publishing software for global brands and agencies. During his tenure at Vitrue, he led a team that worked with many of the world's premier global brands as well as more than 75 agencies worldwide. Among his many industry accolades and awards, Bradford was named one of *Television Week*'s "10 to Watch" for 2005 and one of the "Top 10 Entrepreneurs of the Year" in 2010 by *Business to Business*. He serves on numerous advisory and nonprofit boards, including Bright-Whistle, SoloHealth, and The Brandery.

Sharon Feder
Chief Operating Officer, Mashable

As chief operating officer of Mashable, the leading news site for the connected generation, Sharon Feder oversees all business operations. Since joining Mashable, she has significantly grown the editorial team, extended partnerships with leading news publishers, and created a human resources and recruiting function. During her tenure as publisher, the company has experienced its fastest growth to date and built its own ad sales operations. Feder has held the positions of managing editor and features editor at Mashable and is responsible for building Mashable's native advertising offering. She currently serves on the Social Media Advertising Consortium board and the #GivingTuesday board.

Jason Hirschhorn
Entrepreneur

Jason Hirschhorn is an entrepreneur most comfortable at the intersection between entertainment and technology. Hirschhorn's entry into the tech world came in 1995 when, as a student, he started the website design firm Mischief New Media, purchased five years later by MTV Networks. He eventually became the network's chief digital officer and the youngest senior executive in MTV Networks' history. After MTV, he became president of Sling Media's Entertainment Group, where he led the introduction of Sling's video anywhere device. In 2009, Jason joined MySpace as chief product officer and was named copresident of MySpace a year later. He is currently curator of the widely read Media ReDEFined newsletter.

Andy Markowitz
Director of Global
Digital Strategy, GE

Andy Markowitz leads a global digital strategy group across GE that encourages stakeholder connection and commercial acceleration, employing first-class digital capabilities in areas that include strategy, search, content, social media, and customer engagement. In addition, the group focuses on training and development to help businesses gain marketplace understanding by driving scale, providing external perspective and identifying customer points of relevance. Prior to GE, Markowitz was director of digital services at Kraft Foods, Inc., where he led efforts to create scalable best practices by providing thought leadership in the management and development of a wide range of online marketing principles. He is a frequent industry speaker and was recently named as one of the iIMedia 25: Internet Marketing Leaders and Innovators.

Ted Rubin
Chief Social Marketing
Officer, Collective Bias

Ted Rubin is a leading social marketing strategist, and in March 2009, he started using and evangelizing the term ROR, "return on relationship." It is a concept that he believes is the cornerstone for building an engaged multi-million-member database, many of whom are vocal advocates for the brand, like the one he built for e.l.f. Cosmetics (EyesLipsFace .com) as the chief marketing officer between 2008 and 2010, and for OpenSky, where he was the chief social marketing officer. Rubin sits on several advisory boards, including Blue Calypso, EvenVoice, OpenSky, She-Speaks, Zuberance, and Crowdsourcing Week. His book, *Return on Relationship*, cowritten with Kathryn Rose, was published in 2013.

Herb Scannell
President, BBC Worldwide America at BBC Worldwide

Herb Scannell is responsible for growing the BBC brand and business across all divisions in the United States as well as overseeing the exploitation of BBC Worldwide's global brands. His responsibilities in the United States include cable channel BBC America and BBC Worldwide Productions, BBC.com, sales, and distribution, including digital syndication and motion gallery, home entertainment, and licensed consumer products. As vice chair of MTV Networks and president of Nickelodeon Networks, he oversaw all creative and business operations for a portfolio of brands, including Nickelodeon and TV Land. After MTV Networks, Scannell cofounded and was chief executive officer of Next New Networks, a leading independent producer of online television networks, which was acquired by YouTube/Google in 2011. He has served on the board of directors of several national organizations in the TV industry and public affairs arena, and Help USA, Inc., the nation's largest developer and operator of supportive transitional housing for the homeless.

Rikard Steiber
Global Director of Mobile and Social Ads, Google

Rikard Steiber is a passionate Internet geek and entrepreneur who manages the global marketing team for mobile and social advertising at Google headquarters in California. Before holding this position, he was the European marketing director for all Google products out of London. In his previous career, he founded and managed Digiscope/XLENT Consulting Groups, cofounded Scandinavia Online in Sweden where he was running the portal business, started a multimedia department at Telia, and worked with brand management at Procter & Gamble. He holds a master of science degree from SDA Bocconi School of Management, Milan, Italy, and a bachelor of science degree from Chalmers University of Technology, Gothenburg, Sweden.

The Big Fuel Team

Seth Berk
Chief Marketing Officer, Big Fuel

With nearly 14 years of experience managing sales and marketing initiatives, Seth Berk is a dynamic force behind the open and creative culture at Big Fuel, where he is responsible for driving new business, managing various key partner relationships, and guaranteeing employees' creative expression while producing top-quality work. Prior to joining Big Fuel, Berk was senior vice president of EXPO International, a leading event management company, where he used Facebook and Twitter to boost attendance for EXPO International events. During his 13 years with that company, Berk transitioned the company beyond recruitment events to large-scale automotive and luxury expositions. In addition, he was the prime mover behind the creation of RAND Luxury and the Go Green Expo, which continue to be the key growth drivers to this day.

Nikki Carmel
Group Network
Director, Big Fuel

As group network director, Nikki Carmel currently runs the T-Mobile and Gatorade networks for Big Fuel. Carmel joined Big Fuel from LeadDog Marketing Group in New York City, where for four years she managed experiential, digital, and social marketing campaigns for packaged goods companies, including Seventh Generation, Yes to Carrots, and CLIF Bar. Carmel arrived in New York from Melbourne, Australia, via London. She is adept in client communication, creative problem solving, and social strategy.

Dylan Edgar
Vice President of
Content Production,
Big Fuel

Dylan Edgar supervises campaign deliverables from Content Production, a group comprised of design, technology, and video discipline teams. The production work supports the programs and initiatives of large-brand clients, including T-Mobile, General Motors, Samsung, and Starwood Hotels. Prior to his appointment at Big Fuel, Edgar produced more than 100 hours of long- and short-form content for broadcast TV and the web, and formatted clip shows for more than a dozen networks. In 12 years of media production, Edgar has occupied roles at both large corporate networks and independent production companies. In each environment, his strong work ethic and commitment to high production values resulted in Emmy-nominated work, valuable partnership relationships, and the development of a deep network of industry peers.

Mandy Gresh
Vice President of Brand Channel Management, Big Fuel

Mandy Gresh leads the brand channel management practice at Big Fuel. In this role, she oversees the team of channel and community managers who moderate and produce content for the agency's clients. Prior to Big Fuel, Gresh worked as a digital media and content consultant for such clients as American Express Publishing, the Canadian Tourism Commission, Ladies Who Launch, and Wanderfly. She also spent seven years at Internet media company Travelzoo, including a four-year stint based in Toronto as general manager of its Canadian division.

Mike McGraw
Managing Partner, Big Fuel

At Big Fuel, Mike McGraw oversees content distribution and operations, using his experience with broadcast, online, and mobile platforms to develop effective strategies for clients. Before joining Big Fuel, McGraw founded Link Media Management, a digital content strategy firm that produced high-definition content for pay TV. Prior to Link Media, McGraw worked in Sydney, Australia, heading up broadband content development for Telstra's broadband service. In that role, he oversaw launches of several online services, including Australia's first large-scale music download site, two national sports channels, and the largest online games portal in the Pacific Rim. McGraw also owned and operated Moving Story Pictures, an independent broadcast production company offering programming consulting, production, branding, and other creative services to the pay TV industry.

Michoel Ogince
Director of Platform and Product Strategy, Big Fuel

At Big Fuel, Michoel Ogince leads social labs, the agency's innovation nerve center. Tasked with evaluating emerging social technologies for global Fortune 500 companies, he provides innovative and effective solutions for brands in the social space. Ogince is also founding and managing partner at Windforce Ventures, a venture capital firm specializing in social and mobile technology. He is an advisor at Social iQ Networks, Video Genie, and SocialChorus, and is a frequent speaker at social media technology conferences and events. Ogince was born in South Africa, raised in Australia, and has traversed the globe. He is an ordained rabbi, outdoor enthusiast, avid photographer, and coffee connoisseur.

Anthony Onesto
Chief Talent Officer,
Big Fuel

Anthony Onesto is a talent and operations leader with more than 15 years of staffing, recruitment, and human resources and operational strategy experience. He currently serves as chief talent officer for Big Fuel. In the past, Onesto served as vice president of human resources and then chief operating officer of Zeta Interactive, a leading digital marketing services and technology company. His ability to build fast-growing companies and their human resource functions and to bridge human resource strategy and business is what catapulted him to a senior C-level role in a growing organization.

Josh Scheiner
Vice President of
Content Development
and Distribution,
Big Fuel

As vice president of content development and distribution, Josh Scheiner oversees all social campaigns executed on behalf of Big Fuel's clients, defining a creative vision and determining a distribution strategy for unique and engaging content. In 2007, Scheiner helped cofound Apex Exposure, a forward-thinking digital media and social agency based in New York City. Apex was acquired by Big Fuel in June 2011, when Scheiner was brought on board to lead the agency's distribution department. Once there, he was instrumental in leading the General Motors account, with highlights that included the Sonic 2011 launch and Chevy's 2012 Super Bowl initiatives.

Stuart Schwartzapfel
Vice President of
Audience Insights,
Big Fuel

Stuart Schwartzapfel leads strategic planning, business solutions, and advanced analytics. That means driving content ideation, capitalizing on emerging platform innovation, discovering points of relevance among target audiences, and optimizing owned channel performance for Big Fuel's diverse roster of clients. Prior to joining Big Fuel, Schwartzapfel worked on the agency side in a host of strategic planning and analytics roles for global clients Nissan, Toyota, Lincoln/Mercury, Mahindra, and Mercedes-Benz. He moonlights as an automotive scribe for several internationally syndicated publications, including the *New York Times*, *Autoweek*, and *BusinessWeek*. Schwartzapfel is also a long-standing *Wired* contributor and maintains a popular car-spotting blog called *Man on the Move*.

Christine S. Shoaf
Executive Vice President and Managing Director, Big Fuel

Since 2011, Christine S. Shoaf has been overseeing teams who put out great work, achieved via remarkable creative account service, strategic thinking, and data that drive action. The first "digital native" to run a premier integrated account, AMEX U.S., at Ogilvy and Mather, Shoaf is also credited with heading the most successful product launch in Hanes history, the TAGLESS Tee. She has held positions at various digital agencies, including Jupiter Media Metrix and The Martin Agency, and has experience across many industries, including consumer packaged goods, chemical and science, logistics, automotive, financial services, digital, mobility, social marketing, and technology.

Matt Tepper
Vice President of Audience Insights, Big Fuel

At Big Fuel, Matt Tepper leads a global team focused exclusively on social media marketing. He brings more than 11 years of strategic marketing consulting experience, with expertise spanning marketing strategy, advanced analytics, business innovation, and financial modeling. The fifth person hired to the strategy and analysis practice of Digitas New York in 2002,

Matt was instrumental in helping grow the group to more than 50 professionals in just over four years. Recruited by Company C in 2006 to create and build a similar practice, Tepper successfully developed the capability through an acquisition by Kirshenbaum and Bond. At Kirshenbaum and Bond, he continued to develop the group across broadcast, digital, and social media marketing channels.

FOREWORD

As someone who has piloted corporate digital strategies for more than a decade—first at Kraft Foods and now across GE—I have guided various groups through a wide array of online marketing principles and practices. These days, the question I hear most, whether it is internally, externally, at industry events and trade shows, or in the press, is: How do we tackle social media, and what are the methodologies we need to apply to get our arms around this concept to make sense of it?

I think the first way to respond to such a question is to simply acknowledge that initially, digital (and now social) media fundamentally changed the ways we do business. Critical to effectively dealing with such changes requires that we shift our perspectives to embrace social and digital technology as a driver of business outcomes. If business is about outcomes, digital technology provides both new ways to get to those outcomes as well as a source of new types of outcomes.

Right now, many people and organizations, even those who have been at it for a while, still see social media in very tactical terms. Spend time on any social media publication's website and you are bound to come upon articles and posts offering up a vast menu of tips on how to accomplish just about anything in the social media sphere. These lists may be a surefire way to attract readers, but they rarely result in successful strategies.

There are, however, a growing number of individuals who look beyond the assortment of tools and networks such as Facebook, Twitter, and Pinterest. They recognize, instead, that productive social initiatives call for a more comprehensive, consistent, and long-term approach. Some of these people are the thought leaders Avi Savar has brought together and talked with in putting together this book.

In *Content to Commerce*, one will find ideas that challenge much of the conventional wisdom that has governed marketing for several generations.

Take, for example, the notion that brands and their marketers still control the sales funnel when, in fact, the funnel has been blown up and is being replaced by countless personal funnels that consumers build and control themselves. Each consumer conduit may be completely different from that of one's neighbors, which in turn is different from the people across town, or in the next city, county, or state, or even in other countries, as more and more brands operate on a global scale.

Even more, there is the realization that marketers can no longer lump consumers into traditional demographic categories but instead must see their customers the ways they see themselves, as unique individuals who engage with brands on their own terms, when, where, and how they want.

Granted, these ideas are not radically new. The people you will encounter in these pages have been talking about these issues for some time, but they, and others like them, are still trying to understand how the various parts of the puzzle fit together and what the implications might be.

For those of us who are familiar with both the nuances and hard realities of digital and social media—those of us who have sought to prove its viability—we are moving on to a new stage of accountability. It is now time to step up and say: "It's not the top of the first inning anymore. We have experience. We have learning. We have results. We have smarts. And we are now well into the game."

Nonetheless, there remain those for whom social media marketing is, as my colleague Robert Breese has called it, "a weapon of mass destruction." They still do not get it, and it creates havoc for them. At the other end of the spectrum are "true believers" who see it as a beacon and who readily adopt a series of theoretical methods that have never really been put to the test in the marketplace. In between are practitioners who are at once excited and judicious about social media. For them, social as a term has taken them as far as it can. With respect to the concept, they are asking themselves, What is it we need to do to take it to the next level?

For many, the answer is to focus on content, which is fast becoming social media's currency. As audiences fragment and platforms and channels expand, however, content varies. There is the type of content for which attention is fleeting, its effect minimal. Then there is the stuff you will come back to and the even more compelling stuff that you want to interact with and share. There also are the distinctions between paid, owned, and earned media and how to experiment with them to achieve value, whether to gain awareness or drive engagement over time.

Not only every marketing team, but every other part of every organization, will eventually have to face these critical challenges. This book helps brands meet these challenges by providing a truly unique perspective on the role of social media that elevates the conversation from what has become the conventional concept of "brand as publisher" to the perception that companies must now think of themselves as entire networks.

Much like the best-known brands in the TV business, organizations of every kind must learn to manage multiple channels, developing and delivering specific messages to targeted audiences while simultaneously bringing it all together to create real value through an overarching framework. Through compelling discussions about programming and running the network with the right talent, techniques, and tools, Savar, members of his team, and a diverse array of thought leaders demonstrate how to establish comprehensive social media strategies.

I hope *Content to Commerce* will be the first of many in a line of books that show brands how to build the kinds of models that will enable them to make sense of social media. Such books are key, not just in helping individual businesses address tactical issues, but in helping entire industries identify and understand the opportunities and obstacles so that they can continually adapt and grow. The more books like this one, with great insights and ideas, the faster digital and social media will be established as truly relevant drivers of commercial success.

—Andy Markowitz
Director, Global Digital Strategy
GE

PREFACE

Eureka moments are rare. What is more, they do not usually arrive in a flash. Instead, they often germinate for a long time—possibly years—before they finally surface full-blown.

A Little History

Prior to 2004, I had spent my entire professional career creating and packaging content for some of the biggest and best-known TV broadcasters in the world. That was my day job. The rest of the time I was a technology geek and, by some definitions, an "early adopter." Since the days of CompuServe, Prodigy, and eventually America Online (AOL), I was fascinated by the notion of convergence. In the back of my mind I knew that it was just a matter of time before almost all content would go digital and portable. I just did not know exactly how or when.

By 2004, it was evident that I wasn't the only person thinking this way. A great many of us were not only consuming vast amounts of content online, but producing and sharing much of it as well. I knew that we were moving toward an era when the demand for digital would explode, and as a seasoned TV producer, I had enough credibility to help lead the charge. My approach was quite simple: Leverage new technology and cutting-edge production techniques to make high-quality, low-cost digital content for brands and publishers.

In May 2004, I incorporated Savar Media LLC. Armed with a laptop, a used Sony PD150 Mini DVCAM video camera, and a copy of Final Cut software (a start-up cost of less than $5,000), I was in business. Those were the days when portals like AOL, MSN, and Yahoo! ruled the web. Social media, for the most part, did not exist.

My first two clients were also former college buddies. Both of them ran their own event marketing companies. The jobs were small, but the lessons learned were considerable: Marketing and digital content tasted great together!

Within six months, I was doing work for some terrific people at AOL, which, by then, was dominating the digital content space and pioneering web video. During the next year, we created more than 100 "webisodes" (before they were even called webisodes). Savar Media produced new content formats such as AOL Sessions, launched global content franchises such as Acceso Total, and developed the first forms of branded content with the Chevy Backstage Pass.

Content to Commerce

Propelling these efforts, and many others to follow, were two key drivers—marketing and entertainment—and Savar Media found itself at the center of a rapidly changing digital content landscape. The crew had become experts at filling a gap between brands, agencies, and publishers. Over the next several years, we also became part of a revolution that shaped the emergence of new forms of consumer engagement, branded content, and, ultimately, social marketing. We created branded reality shows, user-generated content programs, influencer programs, casual games, apps, videos, and more. Indeed, we were among the first to create breakthrough content formats that have since become standard practice.

By early 2007, social networks were "crossing the chasm," and audiences were flocking to them in droves. At the same time, portals were losing market share, as search became the gateway to content. Social networks were how more and more consumers were sharing information, however, and the battle cry among advertisers was, "Go viral!"

Although Savar Media had a solid reputation as a content production studio—and close to all its revenue came from producing content—it had begun to provide consulting, planning, and strategic services for free as a way to get in on bigger production budgets. What we at Savar Media soon realized, however, was that these services were just as valuable, if not more so, than the production work itself.

At that point, the production business was also getting increasingly competitive and commoditized. Even as the company grew, so did the number of "preditors" (producer/editors) who had Final Cut at home.

It was easier than ever for just about anyone with the right skills to produce good, low-cost content. So, I decided to dramatically pivot the company.

In 2008, we reworked our business model, raised just under half a million dollars from a small group of angel investors, renamed the firm Big Fuel, and positioned ourselves as one of the world's first marketing and communication companies specializing in branded content and social media. There was just one problem: We had launched the company at the depth of the worst financial crisis of our lifetimes. Potential clients were happy to take meetings with us, and although they listened intently to our pitches and loved our concepts, they had nothing in their budgets to spare.

Fortunately, we had some cash in the bank and decided to ride out the bad market. We brought our overhead down as low as was possible and focused on doing great work for the few clients we did have. Whenever possible, I was out there preaching the "content to commerce" gospel that was at the heart of everything we did. Plus, we produced videos, wrote white papers, and told anyone who would listen that consumer engagement was the new seat at the marketing table.

It was tough—very tough. At least a couple of times, we flirted with the possibility of going out of business. Nonetheless, we were convinced that staying in it was the right move. By early 2009, as the business market began to improve, some brands started to recognize that engaging consumers through great content actually was a smart idea. We also continued to build a strong portfolio of case studies and an impressive body of work so that by the time the market was heating up again in 2010, we were ready to be a leader in branded content and social marketing.

Two years after gambling on our future, we began to make a name for ourselves with some big clients like Colgate-Palmolive and Fisher-Price. Of course, like most small agencies, we were also in perpetual "pitch mode," hoping to score with more brands interested in our nontraditional marketing approach. Little did we know that there was an elephant lurking nearby.

Bagging the Elephant

In early 2010, I was in Los Angeles giving a presentation on branded content best practices, and I happened to connect with a midlevel digital marketing manager from the Hyundai Motor Company. He was thinking about developing a branded app for the company and was intrigued by what I had to say. Not long after, I found myself making the case in front of some of the automaker's top marketing executives. What followed was a series of more meetings, phone calls, and still more meetings until my partner, Mike McGraw, and I wound up in the office of Hyundai's then-marketing head Joel Ewanick. After some light sparring with Ewanick and his lieutenants on the value of social media and the importance of engaging consumers, he turned to his team and ordered: "Let's do it. Go."

Having just landed one of the fastest-growing car companies in the world as a client, we were ecstatic. But our joy was short lived. Just 48 hours after green-lighting the project, Ewanick had jumped to Nissan Motors. Hyundai assured us that the project was still a "go," but just a much slower "go." As we waded through a morass of procurement, scoping, planning, and more procurement, however, we got word that Ewanick had jumped again, this time to General Motors (GM). On the day that the Hyundai contract finally hit our in box, I received an urgent voice mail saying, "Don't sign your deal and get to Detroit as soon as possible."

So there we were at GM headquarters making the case yet again, in front of some of the same people, as several of them had followed Ewanick from Hyundai. Not surprisingly, they were still on board with the idea, yet there was no time for a long courtship. There was a contract with Hyundai sitting on my desk back in New York.

"Give us 48 hours," they told us.

"Okay," we said.

Eleven minutes later, as Mike and I were in our car on the way to the airport, my cell phone rang. "You're in."

The Big Leagues

As the social media agency of record for GM, Big Fuel tripled in size in just four months. Scaling up that quickly and managing the company's rocket-ship trajectory was intense (and should probably be the subject of an entirely different book on business management and operations). We knew everything there was to know about social media, branded content, and consumer engagement, but when it came to playing in the brand and agency big leagues, we were clueless. True, we had experience working with large companies, but GM was a giant global organization with many layers and a mode of operation we had never encountered before.

Moreover, we served the needs of multiple divisions: Chevy, Buick, GMC, and Cadillac. Ewanick sat atop the pyramid, but we essentially had four separate clients, each of which had its own needs, personalities, and priorities, not to mention various creative agencies and partners. Separately, they presented unique challenges. Together, they presented a set of complexities that would challenge even the most seasoned agencies. In the end, it took nearly four months working closely with GM's most senior marketing executives to put together a staffing and resource plan that could handle what was required to service America's top automaker.

By the start of 2011, we had an army of experts in place, with one battalion on the ground in Detroit and another based in Big Fuel's New York headquarters. Despite this arrangement, it soon became abundantly clear that all the internal workflows, processes, and methodologies had to evolve quickly. We needed to adapt to doing business with a giant global organization, integrate with a roster of larger and more conventional agencies, and reframe our products and services around delivering enterprise social media, all on a massive scale.

During the next 18 months, we developed a solid framework for delivering social media, at scale, for large and often intricate brands. It has since become a model that supports the needs of global chief marketing officers and still serves the day-to-day priorities of midlevel brand managers. In addition, it is a way of working that addresses the complexities of collaborating with multiple agencies and integrating across multiple internal departments. As a method of aligning paid, earned, and owned media, it is also a means to deliver tangible value for brands while aligning with their existing metrics for success.

In short, it was during this time that the "network model" was born. Eureka!

ACKNOWLEDGMENTS

This work would not exist without the incredible men and women at Big Fuel. From the leadership team to our coordinators and everyone in between, Big Fuel has assembled the finest collection of people in the industry. They are my colleagues, my friends, and my extended family. I am grateful for all they do, every day.

One person above all has been a sounding board, the brake to my accelerator and a true friend over the years. I might have founded Big Fuel in 2004, but it was when Mike McGraw became my partner a few years later that our true journey began. Thank you, Mike, for all you do.

As any entrepreneur will tell you, most people are happy to see you fail. Still, there are always a few key people who see something unique and decide to take a chance on you. My best friends, Matt Britton and Jeff Frumin, went from being fraternity brothers to becoming my first clients. Ann Boyd was single-handedly responsible for making sure everyone at AOL knew who I was and then doing it again at MySpace a few years later. Angel Sepulveda is the craziest and most fun client anyone could ask for. Scott Campbell and Mindel Klein had the vision and courage to shake things up. And I will be forever indebted to Liz Boone. She took a big chance on a small agency, and I am so proud of what we accomplished together. She changed my life forever.

I would never have been able to pivot Big Fuel and ultimately ride out the financial crisis without the support of my angels. They call them angels for a reason! Alex Fisher, Peter May, Arthur Spector, Mike Emmerman, Andy Appelbaum, Cliff Sirlin, David Karp, Seymour Zises, and Kenny and Leah Daniel all believed in me even though I was speaking a completely different language. Thank you for supporting my crazy ideas!

Along the way three men became my mentors, advisors, and friends: Jordan Rednor, Bob Meyers, and Amir Akhavan—the three wise men.

There is no way I could have survived the emotional roller coaster that consumed my life for years without their help, guidance, and support.

A very special thank-you to my writing partner, Howard Gross, who did so much heavy lifting on this book. It was not an easy project, and I am grateful for his resolve and dedication in helping us get to the finish line.

I also want to thank the entire Social Media Advertising Consortium and my fellow board members for contributing and supporting this project. You are an amazing group of people, and I am honored to call you my colleagues and friends.

Most important, I am who I am today because of my family. My wife, Leigh, and my daughter, Evie, are my rock and my light. It is those two who make everything possible and meaningful in my life. Thank you with all my heart.

INTRODUCTION

C hances are that if you have started to read this book, you may be among the more than 90 percent of marketers who believe that the use of social media is irrevocably changing how consumers interact with brands and that you have no choice but to substantially alter your marketing strategies.[1]

Or maybe you work on the agency side and are attempting to integrate social media with your traditional and digital services. However, the process of creating the kinds of engaging communications that social media demands is turning out to be a lot harder than you thought.

Perhaps you are still in school studying marketing, public relations, or communications and realize what many of your predecessors are first learning on the job: knowing how to manage social channels and platforms is critical to your future success. Indeed, when LinkedIn polled more than 550 business professionals and asked what class would help them most if they could go back to college, one in three answered, "advanced social media skills."[2]

Then again, you might just work at one of the dwindling number of large organizations that have yet to embrace social marketing, but are considering it and hope to avoid many of the mistakes made by earlier adopters.

Whatever your reason, you likely recognize social media's capacity to fuel stronger relationships between companies and consumers, and you are looking to get better at it. The question is how to best do that.

Getting Up to Speed

Although most businesses today attempt to connect with consumers on consumers' terms, many are still ill prepared to do so effectively.

According to research by IBM, nearly 80 percent of companies surveyed have a presence on at least one social network and are aggressively launching social initiatives, with their primary focus on marketing.[3] Yet only about half of these organizations provide their employees with the appropriate training.

The situation is not much better at the nation's colleges and universities. Although the number of institutions offering social media curricula—from community colleges to business schools at prestigious universities such as Harvard, Dartmouth, and Columbia—is increasing, a study of enrolled students or graduates by *U.S. News and World Report* found that 55 percent rated such coursework either "not up to par with the growing industry" or simply unavailable.[4]

The upshot, then, is that it is still largely up to you to further improve your social media knowledge and skills. To that end, you may already have worked your way through several books that offered top-level insights into the power and impact of social media. Now, though, you are ready for a more practical blueprint that will actually guide you through the process—from big-picture strategy to the necessary tactics and tools—to achieve tangible business results.

The Fundamentals

Taking full advantage of the benefits of social media not only entails developing new skill sets, it also requires adopting new mind-sets. In other words, you have to learn to think differently about almost every part of the communication process.

So where do you start?

- First, you must truly understand your audience by listening to their expressed needs, wants, interests, and concerns from within the social space.
- Next, you build an established platform through which you can connect with audiences by generating valuable ideas, an acknowledged voice, and an actionable game plan that give your brand a unique social identity.
- Moreover, you recognize that the traditional models that once sorted content into separate buckets of paid, earned, and owned media are becoming meaningless because audiences ignore these distinctions in favor of seeking out whatever information best serves their needs.

- With that knowledge, you consistently create cross-discipline, cross-platform, and cross-channel programs that reach people when, where, and how they want to be reached.
- You then regularly measure the outcomes and continually improve the process.

These principles may seem basic, but for many brands, adequately executing against them remains a formidable challenge. In some instances, brands steadfastly cling to conventional marketing methods that fall flat in a social environment. Then there are those who are quick to jump on almost any proffered social solution, without first understanding its possible effect or implications.

Success, however, rests somewhere in between.

The Network Model

"Old" media are not going away. In fact, people watch as much TV today as ever before, and the vast majority of it is still viewed on ordinary TV sets.[5] Although newspapers are wilting in the United States and Europe, they are still flourishing in many parts of the world, reaching more than 2 billion people daily, or about 20 percent more than the 1.5 billion who are attracted to social media.[6]

According to Riepl's law (coined by German newspaperman Wolfgang Riepl in 1913), existing media do not disappear when something newer, and possibly better, comes along. Instead, they survive by adopting different formats. Early TV was filled with the kinds of dramas, situation comedies, variety entertainment, and game shows that had previously been staples on radio. As a result, radio became home to talk and a new sensation called "rock 'n' roll." For its part, the Internet has not extinguished any of its predecessors. It is, however, forcing several of them to adjust, and although some forms of marketing will no longer serve you in a socially connected world, others are based on core concepts of communication that will endure change.

One confirmed approach to engaging consumers across social media is to think like a publisher and act like a TV network executive. At Big Fuel, this strategy is known as the network model; it leverages publishing and media techniques to enhance social marketing operations in all types of organizations.

The network model is part Madison Avenue and part Hollywood. It is a comprehensive strategic framework that bridges the gap between the kinds of information, ideas, and entertainment that audiences care most about (content) and a brand's goal of selling its products or services (commerce).

In many ways, it is akin to a broadcast executive's mode of programming, and often it starts with the same questions: Which audience? What channel? At what time will you engage with the most appropriate audience? With what type of content? And can you move them from channel to channel with complementary programming?

Whereas the broadcast network method targets the world, so to speak, by attempting to reach the greatest number of viewers, the social network model focuses on a specific audience and on its specific conversations. As the conversations change, so does the content, not just by the hour or the day, but over the course of an entire year or more.

Moreover, even as brands increasingly recognize the value of targeting specific audiences and conversations on different channels, they typically deal with each channel independently. The network model, however, is designed to provide a strategic framework for thinking about how various channels, along with different tools, techniques, and talent, work together to collectively enhance a brand.

Thus, it is possible to consistently develop cross-channel programs that reach people where they want to be reached, with content that is relevant to them, across the channels where they spend their time, all the while creating greater value.

Higher Highs and Higher Lows

A traditional media and promotional flow looks somewhat like a hospital heart rate monitor, with hills and valleys emerging around media investment and attrition (Figure I.1). When a brand spends money to build awareness as part of a campaign or leading up to an event, the rate ascends. Once the event has occurred or the media investment has ended, it descends. Over the course of a campaign, this cycle may be repeated over and over.

Although it is medically unwise to keep a patient's heart rate at peak levels—and financially impractical to maintain a campaign's high level of spending—over an extended period, there are ways to keep either from flatlining.

In the case of spending, the value of a brand's network can significantly alter the dynamic of its "heart rate" by allowing paid, owned, and

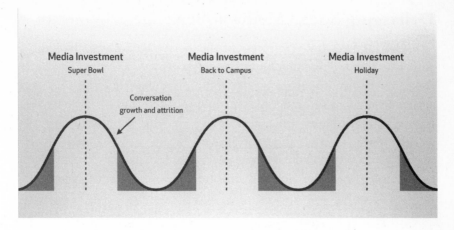

Figure I.1 Traditional Media and Promotional Flow

earned media to work together. Rather than simply relying on paid media to fuel a campaign, owned and earned media can be used to extend its life by continually identifying an audience's needs and interests; generating new and better ideas to address them; cultivating advocates and influencers; and establishing meaningful, long-term relationships. All come with the goal of boosting each peak to drive "higher highs" and sustaining each valley to deliver "higher lows" (Figure I.2).

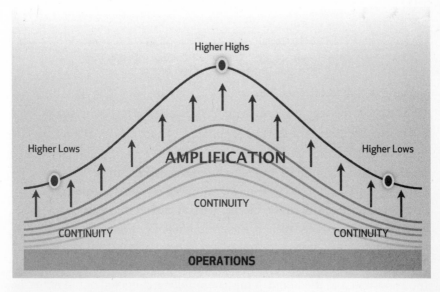

Figure I.2 Higher Highs and Higher Lows

Delivering Social Media at Scale

What has just been described is essentially social media at scale. By putting audiences first and building multichannel strategies and campaigns, social media operations can attain greater and more extensive reach than they could through more traditional techniques. The cumulative effect of driving "higher highs and higher lows" is what ultimately creates a valuable network effect (Figure I.3). The "heart rate" begins to tilt and the value of the overall network increases. For its part, the network model is designed to achieve this by delivering against three key objectives: amplification, continuity, and operations.

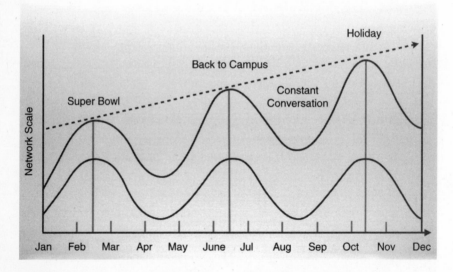

Figure I.3   The Network Effect

Amplification

Consumers' relationships with brands no longer end at the point of purchase. Indeed, long after buying a product or service, consumers may continue to engage with the brand, actively promoting or assailing it via social media channels. When handled correctly, this interaction often enables a two-way conversation, which in turn allows for more personalized communication and, ultimately, engenders a sense of trust between the consumer and the brand. Thus, a carefully architected brand network can help amplify everything a brand does or says in the marketplace, with the goal of maximizing paid media to drive earned media and build owned media.

Continuity

It is not uncommon for a series of tweets to be converted into a Facebook page if the subject has generated considerable interest or for a comment to someone's post to become the basis of a blog post of its own. These connections are examples of continuity, and brands can participate in this process by producing their own posts and responses and by providing "always-on" channel management. When distinct channels are in sync and working together, it is possible to keep conversations going over long periods and to connect the dots between paid-media flights even after an event has ended or when there is no longer a campaign in market.

Operations

If you think about operations in terms of a TV network, it is the equivalent of a network operations center, which exists to ensure that the lights stay on, the machines are humming, the satellites are responding, and all forms of content run on time. A successful social network must also be operationally sound. It must function like a well-oiled machine in which the right talent along with the right tools, techniques, and processes work together to produce optimum results.

What Is a Network?

A network is essentially a brand's collection of owned media channels: its Facebook page, YouTube channel, Twitter feed, Tumblr blog, and so forth. Each channel needs to be programmed independently to drive the goals of the entire network forward.

Today, marketers often ask the question, What are we doing on Facebook? The more appropriate question, however, is What is Facebook doing for our network? Long-term success comes at the network level, not among individual channels. How brand channels are made to work alongside paid media—so as to successfully drive earned and build owned media—is at the core of the network model (Figure I.4). The

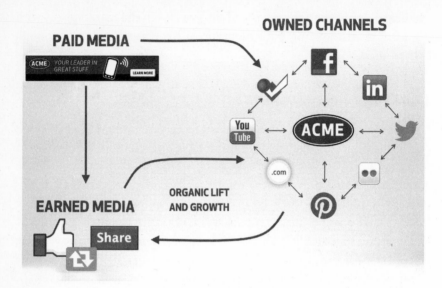

Figure I.4   Leveraging Paid Media to Drive Earned and Build Owned Media

objective is to drive efficiencies across all channels while also addressing the key challenges that most organizations regularly face.

Alignment

To take full advantage of paid-media dollars and make the most of existing opportunities, it is essential that there is a mechanism for aligning all elements of a campaign around what matters most to its audience. One of the best ways to do so is to focus on cultural "water cooler moments" that can yield high-volume consumer conversations. In marketing speak, they are known as tent poles.

On TV, a tent-pole event is a type of top-rated program whose popularity can carry over to shows that follow it. A classic example is the strategy of premiering a new network series right after the Super Bowl. Online, tent poles may manifest themselves as large media buys or cultural events of relevance that provide ideal opportunities for brands to join in large-scale existing conversations. Other examples of tent poles include holidays, major sporting events, movie premieres, and award shows along with new product launches and brand refreshes.

Structure

It is not unusual for brands to deal with multiple events, channels, platforms, and campaigns over the course of a social project and to do so with numerous partners and agencies. For that reason, a comprehensive framework for these separate internal and external resources—both big and small—is critical. A clearly defined programming grid is a way to organize and oversee all the various pieces, players, and activities by providing clarity and a standard by which to communicate across the enterprise (Figure I.5). The programming grid represents a yearlong view of network activities and is aligned with various tent poles and other external events. It tracks daily, weekly, and monthly schedules of network activities, and it informs every part of the process.

Repeatability

With social media still relatively new to so many organizations, how can they drive efficient and consistent results without reinventing the wheel every time? The answer is that organizations can develop and adhere to specific, proven strategic initiatives that are designed to match business challenges—such as increasing sales, improving sentiment, enhancing

Marketing Windows										
		Winter			Spring		Back to School		Fall	
	January	February	March	April	May	June	July	August	September	October
Event Support										
	CES	Grammys		Coachella		E3			Fall Event	
	Sundance					Father's Day				
Pure Social Media Campaigns (Each With Dedicated Media Support)										
Gold/Silver Campaigns	Lumia Launch		Capture Coachella				TBD Execution		TBD Execution	
	Social King of CES				Living in the Mo(ment) Ville Launch					
Advertising Supportive Campaigns				No more Mr Nice Girl					Brand Rerfresh	
Channel Development										
High Effort					YouTube Super Channel					
Medium Effort			FB Timeline Launch	Support Tab	Deals Tab					
Low Effort		Ratings & Reviews	YouTube Channel Launch		FB Profile Swap		FB Profile Swap		FB Profile Swap	
Always On										
			Facebook Media Buys 'Always On' and 'Retention & Engagement'							
			Integration with Customer Facing Business Groups							
			Brand Channel Management							

Figure I.5   The Grid

general branding, and increasing engagement and the number of fans or followers—with clearly defined objectives.

These business solutions include techniques such as leveraging influencers and advocates, facilitating online commerce, and effectively integrating paid, owned, and earned media. They may also feature tools such as video, games, and consumer-generated content. Whatever a brand is trying to accomplish, it can plug in the correct business solution to achieve that. What is more, these solutions are packaged with advanced analytics and metrics, and they are intended to deliver brand value over time.

Discipline

In the social sphere, priorities may need to change as often as content, and frequently what may confront the day-to-day marketing manager may not yet even be on the radar of a chief marketing officer. The challenge is to be able to correlate the needs and concerns of both by understanding what truly matters to their key common interest: their audience.

A brand's priorities—whether emanating top down or bottom up— need to align with its fundamental principles, practices, and goals so as to ensure that it can readily carry out and maintain all three. At the same time, however, its interests also have to square with those of its existing customers as well as with the new consumers it hopes to engage. Therefore, it must sync all these various prerogatives by learning how to take part in conversations that spark audiences' attention and interests.

Putting It All Together

For that reason, the network model is an approach that has no borders. It is, as Seth Berk, chief marketing officer of Big Fuel, says

> completely agnostic in terms of channels, platforms, tools, and techniques, and instead, integrate[s] the various elements as and when appropriate. The model lets you evaluate what you are currently doing as a brand marketer. It lets you take a step back and look at how you're organized, look at how your departments talk to one another, look at how social media lives within your

organization, and get a good understanding of whether you are applying these best practices. And if not, it also highlights the changes you need to make in order to do so.

Unlike more conventional marketing models, which are based on how to map a brand to an audience, the network model takes it a step further and determines how to map a brand to the conversation that audience is having. As the conversations change, no matter how quickly, the strategy can change as well. In addition, because many conversations never really stop, the network model has a cumulative benefit over time, allowing it to continually blossom and grow.

From conceptualizing an idea to fulfilling it across paid, earned, and owned media, the network model provides a clear path to deliver significant and measurable value. Along the way, it also transforms shallow and short-term projects into deep, targeted, long-term engagements. The cumulative effect is that both highs and lows are elevated at the starting point and move forward from there.

In short, the network model is a proven means to navigate today's highly fragmented and hyperconnected terrain. It is what this book is all about.

Notes

1. One study shows that 92 percent of marketers believe that the use of social media has fundamentally changed how consumers engage with brands, and 93 percent believe that marketers need to reinvent their brand-building strategies. NM Incite (citing Forrester Research), "Delivering on the Promise," 2012, http://nmincite.com/wp-content/uploads/2012/07/NM-Incite-White-Paper-Delivering-on-the-Promise.pdf.

2. Kristin Piombino, "If You Could Go Back to School, Which Class Would Help You Most in Your Job Today?" LinkedIn, July 19, 2012, www.linkedin.com/osview/canvas?_ch_page_id=1&_ch_panel_id=1&_ch_app_id=1900&_applicationId=1900&_ownerId=0&appParams={%22section%22:%22results%22,%22poll_id%22:%22347056%22} (original link), www.raganstore.com/PublicRelations/Articles/Poll_Communicators_wish_they_took_a_social_media_s_45145.aspx (available link).

3. IBM Institute for Business Value, "From Social Media to Social CRM: Reinventing the Customer Relationship," June 2011, http://public.dhe.ibm.com/common/ssi/ecm/en/gbe03416usen/GBE03416USEN.PDF.

4. Stacy Blackman, "Social Media Skills a Must for MBAs, Survey Says," *U.S. News and World Report,* September 30, 2011, www.usnews.com/education/blogs/MBA-admissions-strictly-business/2011/09/30/social-media-skills-a-must-for-mbas-survey-says.

5. Although nearly 80 percent of all U.S. Internet users regularly visit social media sites, more than 95 percent of all Americans regularly watch television. "I Want My IPTV! The Growth of the Connected Television," *Nielsen Wire,* August 1, 2012, http://blog.nielsen.com/nielsenwire/media_entertainment/i-want-my-iptv/.

6. Rachel McAthy, "Global Circulation Falls as Readers Become 'Promiscuous,' " *journalism.co.uk,* October 13, 2011, www.journalism.co.uk/news/global-circulation-falls-as-readers-become-promiscuous-/s2/a546340/.

SECTION I

Brand as Network

CHAPTER 1

Beyond Publishing

"Think like a publisher" has become one of the most oft-repeated mantras of the social media movement and for good reason. The average American is exposed to as many as 3,000 marketing messages a day (via commercials, billboards, banner ads, search advertising, logos, and more), a mere fraction of which are of real value to any given person at any given time. Getting someone's attention amid all this noise is a chore. Making an impression is a challenge. Engaging that person for an extended period of time is a truly formidable challenge. All those challenges, though, need to be the ultimate goals of any brand hoping to succeed at social marketing.

By now, most marketers are aware of the challenge. In fact, more than 90 percent of those surveyed by Forrester Research recognize that social media marketing has fundamentally altered the relationship between brands and their customers, forcing marketers to reconstruct their brand-building strategies.[1] The good news is that the tools and techniques already exist to make it happen. The not-so-good news, at least so far, is that many marketers are unprepared to use these assets effectively.

Publisher's Advantage

Publishers are particularly adept at listening to public discourse and understanding how to leverage the popular zeitgeist by piggybacking on what people are thinking and talking about. Sharon Feder, chief operating officer at Mashable.com, is responsible for both building the news website's editorial team and growing its native advertising program, and she believes that this skill is among Mashable's greatest strengths:

> *As publishers we are always creating compelling content because, by default, we have a content frame of mind. We are interested in what people want to know. One of the advantages we have is that we view every person who works at this company as representative of our audience. They are part of the connected generation. They are people who are constantly on their smartphones. They are on any number of social networks, constantly sharing and adopting technology. And so for us, we're able to say to our staff, would this interest you, would this be valuable to you? And I think it really benefits us to have people who can think about and understand our audience and their needs.*

Redefining the Audience

Unfortunately, most brands can't echo Feder's words. In large part, branded content has traditionally been defined as advertising, and most advertising is about driving potential customers to the point of buying a product or service. Social media marketing attempts to reach the same destination, but its itinerary includes building relationships along the way. To do so, marketers must stop thinking of the people they are trying to reach as consumers and regard them instead as members of the audience, the way publishers do. That requires learning how to inform, educate, and entertain. First, though, they have to redefine what it means to be the audience.

With conventional media, the role of the audience has traditionally been a passive one, epitomized by newspaper readers, moviegoers, and, of course, the couch potato in front of the TV set. When it comes to the ever-expanding array of social media, though, the audience's role is anything but inactive. Although people continue to be content consumers, they are also producers, distributors, critics, and, increasingly, competitors. When it comes to getting others to decide on purchasing a product, research has shown that ordinary word of mouth is more likely to move the needle than are many brands.[2] In the realm of social media, the name of the game is neither attention nor impressions, but engagement.

Keeping in Touch

So what do publishers know that many brands still do not?

At the very least, they understand how to keep people up-to-date on matters that are important to them. When asked why they regularly check in with their social networks, 62 percent of participants in a State of Social Media study said that it's because they don't want to miss out on the latest news, events, or status updates.[3] Nearly 40 percent of them said that the need to stay in touch is so great that they would rather do their taxes, run a marathon, get a root canal, or go to jail before giving up their social media profiles.

Such extreme dedication notwithstanding, what keeps many people on social networks is simply the opportunity to interact. Research out of Harvard University's Social Cognitive and Affective Neuroscience Lab, for example, has discovered that sharing information about themselves makes people "feel really good," in much the same way sex does.[4] Similar studies have shown that as many as 80 percent of average users' social media posts are composed of self-disclosure. Moreover, people on social sites often exhibit what Rider University psychology professor John Suler defines as the disinhibition effect,[5] whereby they feel free to divulge very personal things about themselves that they might not be willing to share in other settings.

Albeit to a lesser degree of intimacy, long before the existence of the Internet or social media, newspapers and magazines recognized the value of connecting with stakeholders through op-eds, guest commentaries, and letters to the editor. These days, these media openly encourage readers to comment on stories and even converse directly with writers and reporters. Brands, for the most part, remain reluctant to do so.

Customer service company Genesys found that more than half of consumer-facing Fortune 500 companies suffer from "social shyness," failing to make their social media identities available to their clientele. Fifty-five percent do not list a Twitter handle on their contact page, and 51 percent provide no link to Facebook.[6] More than one in four companies leave no indication of their social media presence anywhere on their websites.

Telling Stories

The ability to tell stories is what sets publishers far apart from most other brands. During the past several years, neuroscientists have begun to appreciate what raconteurs of all kinds have known for a long time: People relate best to stories.[7] Indeed, the narrative is the basic organizing principle of memory and helps people make sense of their worlds. Stories that present information in a compelling fashion or pique emotions are deeply encoded into the mind. And well-told tales are not just remembered, they are believed.

One reason stories work so well is that they entertain. It's no wonder that entertainment-related companies and products generate considerable numbers of "likes" and "follows."[8] Likewise, the types of content that users most respond to on social channels are entertaining by nature: videos, photographs, jokes, and cartoons.

Beyond Publishing

These strategies are but some of the lessons that brands need to learn, but even as companies alter their marketing methods to embrace the notion of thinking as publishers, publishing itself has started to change. Years of reading blogs, Facebook posts, and tweets have made audiences more amenable to less formal styles of writing. At the same time, tools such as WordPress and sites like Tumblr and Svbtle have made it easier to design and manage content.

The emergence of consumer-generated content has also significantly transformed the art of storytelling. In the past, for example, if a newspaper "put a story to bed," it essentially closed the book on it. Now, as more stories are streamed and shared in real time, they are not likely to end until readers have lost all interest. Throughout 2011, several of the biggest news stories of the year—the rise of the Arab Spring, the death of Osama bin Laden, and the earthquake in Japan—were first told, and later spread, via tweets and Facebook posts.

No doubt, brands must change, sometimes dramatically, to keep pace with the kinds of publishers they aspire to emulate, especially those publishers who will, themselves, have to adapt to stay relevant in a real-time, "always-on" marketplace. As Mashable's Feder notes, history suggests that neither is likely to do so easily:

None of the publishers who are household names today built themselves up overnight. They really took a long time to create their offerings and earn brand respect. The same is true of some of the brand names that have become very popular in the social media space. Those are brands that have been working at it for five-plus years. None of those brands established that credibility in social overnight either.

Time may not be on their side as the social space grows larger and ever more complex, however, so much so that it is time for brands to think beyond publishing.

Keep in Mind . . .

1. Although the vast majority of brands recognize that there has been a fundamental change in their relationship with consumers, few have figured out how to adapt.
2. Once-passive audiences are now creating and distributing their own content, sometimes in direct competition with brands.
3. While research has shown that most people use social media to keep in touch with the world around them, half of all brands fail to take advantage of this situation.
4. People not only remember well-told stories, they believe them.
5. Even as brands try to think like publishers, they must realize that publishers themselves are starting to think differently.

Notes

1. NM Incite, "Delivering on the Promise: Five Ways to Drive Brand Effectiveness through Social Media," 2012, http://nmincite.com/wp-content/uploads/2012/07/NM-Incite-White-Paper-Delivering-on-the-Promise.
2. Nielsen Company, "Nielsen: Global Consumers' Trust in 'Earned' Advertising Grows in Importance," 2012, www.nielsen.com/us/en/insights/press-room/2012/nielsen-global-consumers-trust-in-earned-advertising-grows.html.
3. "National Survey Reveals Consumers Are Overwhelmed by Social Media," *BusinessWire*, August 1, 2012, www.businesswire.com/news/home/20120801005524/en/National-Survey-Reveals-Consumers-Overwhelmed-Social-Media.
4. Graeme McMillan, "Over-Sharing on Social Media Is Just Like Sex, Experts Say," *Digital Trends*, May 9, 2012, www.digitaltrends.com/social-media/over-sharing-on-social-media-is-just-like-sex-experts-say/.

5. John Suler, "The Online Disinhibition Effect," *The Psychology of Cyberspace*, accessed October 10, 2012, http://users.rider.edu/~suler/psycyber/disinhibit.html.

6. Genesys, "Genesys Research Finds Big Business Still Uneasy with Customer Service Conversations over Social Media," August 23, 2012, www.genesyslab.com/news -and-events/press-releases/genesys-research-finds-big-business-still-uneasy-with -customer-service-conversations-over-social-media.aspx.

7. Jason Gots, "Your Storytelling Brain," *Big Think*, January 15, 2012, http://bigthink .com/think-tank/your-storytelling-brain.

8. ROI Research, "Life on Demand: Participant Behavior and Social Engagement," *SlideShare*, July 25, 2012, www.slideshare.net/performics_us/performics-life-on -demand-2012-summary-deck.

CHAPTER 2

Social Media Is an Octopus

In the classic Indian tale of the elephant and the blind men, several sightless wanderers come upon an elephant for the first time. In trying to determine what it is, each man touches a different part of the animal. To one fellow who grasps the trunk, it is a squirming snake. To another who holds the tail, it is a rope. For a third who falls against its side, it is like a wall, and so on for each wanderer. Not only do their various perceptions lead them to quarrel, but they also fail to accurately identify the beast.

Such is currently the case with social media. Practices as diverse as marketing, public relations, customer service, and even crisis management claim it as part of their domains. Traditional creative agencies may see it as a funny video spot on YouTube. Public relations professionals would argue that it is all about influencer outreach. Customer service might say it is just another form of customer relationship management. And to some degree they would all be right.

As social media quickly expands across the enterprise and beyond, it touches just about every facet of business, making it more analogous to an octopus than an elephant (Figure 2.1). Indeed, it is becoming ubiquitous both inside and outside just about any type of organization, and it is driving change throughout the entire business process.

Consider, for example, some of the different disciplines social media affects.

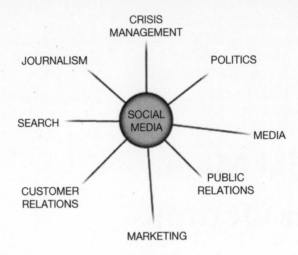

Figure 2.1   The Social Media Octopus

Marketing

In the United States, 9 out of 10 marketing professionals are using some form of social media in their work. That is a significant jump from 2008, when barely 20 percent were doing so.[1] Worldwide, more than half of all social media initiatives at large companies are aligned to marketing.[2] Not surprisingly, then, advertising is the single largest generator of social media revenue and is rapidly approaching the $10 billion mark.[3]

In terms of both time and money, such investments are paying off. In an Economist Intelligence Unit survey of more than 300 senior managers at firms across North America, 84 percent of executives said their social media campaigns had improved their marketing and sales efforts, while 81 percent credited social media with increasing their market share.[4] In fact, respondents whose companies had established a considerable presence on social sites reported an average return on investment that was more than four times what nonsocial companies had experienced.

Despite their overwhelming approval of social media, however, many practitioners are still plagued by a sense of uncertainty regarding their social prowess. According to a joint study by Unilever and Silverman Research, the number-one barrier hindering brands from using social media is a lack of knowledge about how to effectively implement it in practical terms (see Figure 2.2).[5] Following this are factors such as the

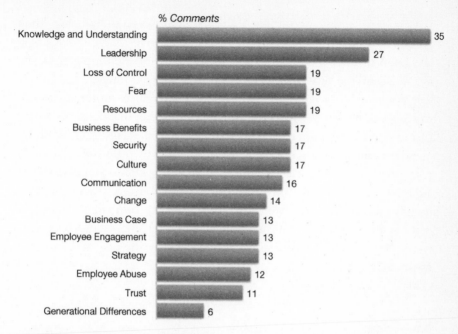

Figure 2.2 Main Barriers for Organizations in Embracing Social Media Practices

inability to control the communication process and the absence of a comprehensive social strategy. Consequently, even among socially savvy brands, there can still be a significant learning curve.

Customer Relations

The brands that have made it to the top of the hill have begun to realize that social marketing is more than simply a new way of selling their products and services. Just as important, it is also a means to build long-term relationships with customers. Although most companies still consider raising brand awareness and reputation as their top social priorities, many are increasingly turning their attention to relationship management. A global study of marketing and communication executives presented by FedEx and advertising agency Ketchum found that slightly more than half believe they are already particularly effective at strengthening relationships with customers and the public in general.[6]

Granted, companies have always sought ways to enhance their connection with consumers, but social media presents new challenges and opportunities. To start, the very nature of the relationship is changing as the balance of power shifts to customers who no longer have to rely solely on brands to provide information and, even more important, insights about their products. By now, it is no secret that consumers trust recommendations from friends and family above all forms of advertising.[7]

Consumers also expect companies to genuinely listen and accurately respond to their needs and desires; thanks to recent advances in data collection and analysis, this expectation coincides nicely with business interests. In fact, research from IBM has shown that more than 70 percent of C-level executives worldwide want to better understand their customers on an individual level, and then develop the means to become more responsive.[8] To that end, more than half anticipate that social channels will be the primary way to do so.

Conversation

How does social media influence the role of customer relations within organizations?

Pete Blackshaw, global head of digital and social media, Nestlé: "Social media starts with consumer services, because a good service experience or bad service experience amplifies really well. Plus, it's the hardest consumer motion, and I think that we need to build operations that really put a whole new value on consumer motions."

Rikard Steiber, global marketing director of mobile and social advertising, Google: "In things like customer service, social can play a much more important role than we perhaps think today. You don't necessarily need to go into a call center. You can leverage your customers who may be peers or experts and who actually know things in various forms."

Reggie Bradford, senior vice president of product development, Oracle: "If they have a complaint, like their flight is delayed or they check into a hotel and there's something wrong with the bed, they don't necessarily call the front desk. In many cases they will just complain on the brand page or a social channel, where they can amplify that complaint across lots and lots of customers."

Jason Hirschhorn, owner, ReDEF Group: "The tables have turned from waiting on a customer service line and being transferred to all these different lines and maybe never get [ting] anywhere, to brands being so afraid of negative sentiment that they do deal with you very quickly. The brands that just say 'sorry' don't help. Customer service is about accountability, action, and outcome, not about 'sorry.'"

Public Relations

Of all the disciplines affected by social media, none should (at least in theory) be better prepared to handle it than public relations. Unlike advertisers and conventional agencies, who have grown comfortable with their ability to control every aspect of the marketing message, public relations professionals know what it is like to release content into the wild and watch as it is remolded, manipulated, and sometimes distorted. Nonetheless, many PR pros are also struggling to adapt.

In some cases, public relations has surrendered its lead to a new breed of marketers who understand the social worth of branded content. Whether constructing a 140-character tweet, a brief post, or a much longer blog, more and more content marketers are starting to appreciate the importance of good storytelling. Those who can't master the art have begun to compete with public relations firms for the talents of professional journalists who have either abandoned or been jettisoned from traditional news outlets. And because most consumers do not discern the difference between marketing and public relations, it matters little to them where relevant content comes from.

Public relations is also coming to terms with social media being a more measurable form of media, and PR practitioners have to identify the appropriate methods and metrics for gauging the value of their work. In 2010, the profession took an initial step forward with its declaration of the Barcelona Principles,[9] a set of seven criteria for guiding and evaluating public relations. It was followed in 2012 by the creation of the first social media measurement standards (#SMMStandards), which, in the words of its founders, will "accelerate the shift from low-level counting to higher-level value."[10]

Also in 2012, the Public Relations Society of America updated the definition of public relations to something more aligned with the age of social media. The result was the following statement: "Public relations is a strategic communication process that builds mutually beneficial relationships between organizations and their publics."[11] No doubt there will still be more to add to that.

Crisis Management

Once considered a subset of public relations, crisis management has moved up and to the forefront of PR. Often, crises are defined by two crucial factors: speed and control. In many instances, social media has considerably accelerated the former and dramatically reduced the latter. In the summer of 2012, for example, with Syria in a state of near civil war, a tweet supposedly posted from the account of Russian Interior Minister Vladimir Kolokoltsev announced that Syrian President Bashar al-Assad had been killed (Figure 2.3). Within just 16 minutes, the price for light, sweet crude-oil futures jumped a dollar on world markets. Even after the rumor had been squelched and the matter was under control, oil closed on the New York Mercantile Exchange at the highest settlement price in nearly a month.

Figure 2.3 Twitter Posting

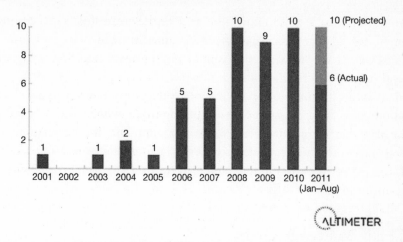

Figure 2.4   Annual Occurrence of Social Media Crises (2001 through 2011)

Data: 50 social media crises occurring between January 2001 and August 2011.

With the advent of social media, inaccurate data and misinformation have seemingly spread across the Internet before anyone has had the opportunity to even think "Oops," and the number of critical situations has been on the rise. After analyzing 50 social media crises that have occurred since 2001, the research and advisory firm Altimeter Group found that the number of incidents has risen steadily, from one or two predicaments per year during the first 5 years to a total of 10 such events in 2010 alone[12] (Figure 2.4). Moreover, the crises studied tended to be platform agnostic. They originated almost evenly across Facebook, Twitter, YouTube, blogs, and communities.

Journalism

The changes wrought by social media on marketing and public relations are also reflected in the current state of journalism. Consumers today regularly bypass mainstream news outlets to find out what is going on in the world. Twitter is frequently the first to break major news stories, as was the case with the Hudson River plane crash, the announcement of Britain's royal wedding, and the death of Osama bin Laden. More

Americans also rely on YouTube as a principal platform for viewing news, a third of which is produced by other citizens.[13]

The rise of social media and the subsequent need for real-time reporting has forced the Fourth Estate to rethink its policies and practices. Many news organizations now allow—and in some cases require—their reporters to blog, post, and tweet in addition to their normal chores. Reuters, which maintains a team of social media editors to fact-check tweets in real time, permits its reporters to tweet first and file a story after. Other news operations are turning part of their work over to nonprofessionals. CNN's iReport website has allowed more than 750,000 people to volunteer and submit stories from every point on the globe.

Fast is not always synonymous with factual or intelligible, though, and the ascendency of consumer-generated content has not diminished the need for someone to manage, verify, and make sense of it all. Where editors once typified this responsibility, individuals and organizations are now taking on the role. Aggregation apps like Flipboard, Pulse, and Zite collect and organize stories from both traditional and social sources. Social news sites such as reddit and Newsvine go a step further by allowing readers to identify articles and share them with friends, while Storify and Summify let users assemble material from various social networks to create their own reports.

The good news for news organizations is that, according to Pew Research Center's Project for Excellence in Journalism, a much smaller percentage of American adults get their news through social networks like Facebook and Twitter (9 percent) than directly from the organizations' websites (36 percent).[14] The not-so-good news is that a growing number of consumers are using "news-organizing" websites (29 percent). Realizing that they may no longer be able to "beat 'em" when it comes to competing with citizen journalists to be the first to break news—or with aggregators and curators as the first means to deliver it—more and more organizations are deciding to "join 'em" by seeking new opportunities.

Media

Learning to "join 'em" rather than "beat 'em" has been a hard lesson for some in the media business. Throughout much of the past decade, the Recording Industry Association of America (RIAA) waged a legal battle with music fans, filing more than 30,000 suits against peer-to-peer file sharers, almost all of which have since been settled out of court. Around the same time, a consortium of independent filmmakers launched its own RIAA-style litigation campaign, specifically targeting thousands of "movie pirates" who used the BitTorrent file-sharing protocol to download their work.

Television executives, too, were initially inclined to fight back when confronted with the same dilemma. But to Jason Hirschhorn—formerly president of Sling Media's Entertainment Group, where he led the introduction of the Slingbox video anywhere device, and now the owner of the ReDEF Group and curator of Media ReDEFined—the idea that television networks were upset because people were clipping their shows and sharing them on YouTube makes little sense:

> *If someone is clipping your show, think what kind of evangelist he or she is. Through technology, they can pass that around, which is free marketing that you would otherwise have had to pay for. And it is trackable. So letting people have more of a conversation around your content and making it more shareable means it is probably going to be seen by more people. And that is the greatest marketing you could have.*

Indeed, although the vast majority of Americans still watch television the old-fashioned way—on conventional TV sets—they can hardly be called couch potatoes anymore. Moreover, the term *watch* may no longer apply to a growing segment of the television audience. More than half of all mobile phone owners of adult age use them in one way or another while in front of their TVs.[15] Smartphones, and even smarter tablets, are creating a culture of what Pew Research has dubbed connected viewers, who share text messages with friends during the course of a TV show, visit sites that have been mentioned on air, verify information they may have seen or heard, or while away the time during commercial breaks.

Helping make the experience easier and more enjoyable are a host of apps like IntoNow, Shazam, and Viggle, which enable audiences to tweet with their favorite actors, connect to special offers, and earn loyalty points that can be redeemed for prizes. In the months leading up to the 2012 presidential election, the specially designed Super PAC App made it possible for viewers watching political advertising to identify who

Male		Female	
1. Doritos	86,194	1. Sun Drop	177,099
2. M&M's	83,499	2. M&M's	129,671
3. Sun Drop	77,605	3. Doritos	108,932
4. Pepsi	72,444	4. Pepsi	93,832
5. McDonald's	64,971	5. McDonald's	76,805
6. Geico	58,645	6. Geico	68,966
7. Google	56,686	7. Burger King	50.594
8. Chevrolet	53,249	8. Google	42,604
9. Kia	46,480	9. Weight Watchers	42,193
10. Nike	46,319	10. Wheat Thins	41,825

Figure 2.5   Top 10 Brands among U.S. Females versus Males, Ranked by Number of Social Media Comments,* H1 2012

Note: Mentions on public Twitter and Facebook accounts; *comments made about commercials.

Source: Bluefin Labs, July 9, 2012.

financed an ad and how much it cost. In addition, they could go online and fact-check the content.

These tools have greatly expanded the conversations before, during, and after television programs. In the first half of 2012, viewers engaged in more than 350 million interactions on channels like Twitter, Facebook, and GetGlue, all related to television programming.[16] To the delight of many brands, they also discussed the most popular commercials, although women far outnumbered men in this activity (Figure 2.5).

As socializing the television experience becomes a national pastime, viewers are using it to spend more time focused on other popular diversions, such as baseball, football, basketball, and, in 2012, the Summer Olympics. The 2012 games generated a record-breaking 150 million tweets, which reached a pace of 80,000 a minute following Jamaican Usain Bolt's 200-meter gold-medal-winning sprint. In total, Bolt garnered more than 960,000 mentions across social networks, considerably ahead of the 830,000 mentions for American swimmer Michael Phelps.[17] At the same time, the number of Facebook fans of American gymnast Gabby Douglas grew nearly fourfold during the two-week period.

Along with other tent-pole events such as the Super Bowl, the World Series, the NBA Finals, and nonsports celebrations like the Oscars and the Grammy Awards, social television provides a unique opportunity to share important experiences with millions of consumers.

Politics

Perhaps the single biggest competitive event in 2012 to capture the attention and interest of social media users was the presidential election. The photo of Barack and Michelle Obama hugging, under text that read "Four More Years," became the most retweeted post ever and capped a year in which social became a critical part of politics. (Obama also received congratulatory tweets from a host of world leaders, including David Cameron, prime minister of the United Kingdom; Julia Gillard, prime minister of Australia; and Mohd Najib Tun Razak, prime minister of Malaysia.)

Both presidential candidates, along with scores of other politicians running for national, state, and local positions, relied more on social media than at any time in the past. Obama, who was already a veteran user from the 2008 race, relied heavily on Twitter to sometimes bypass the filters of traditional media during the campaign. He also held a surprise "Ask Me Anything" chat on social news site reddit that attracted more than 3 million page views and more than 23,000 comments. Along with Republican opponent Mitt Romney, the president sent a slew of messages to voters throughout Election Day, urging supporters to turn out for what was expected to be a very tight race. Even after the election, Obama has continued to rely on the reach of social sites to garner support around issues such as the fiscal cliff.

Elected officials, however, were not the only ones to take to social sites to enhance the democratic process. According a Pew Research Center report released shortly after the election, thousands of Facebook users who affixed an "I Voted" button to their newsfeeds helped drive an additional third of a million people to polling places.[18] What is more, those users were able to keep score by viewing a real-time map that carried a running total of Facebook-tracked voters, including such information as gender, age, and geographic location. The Pew report also found that, in true social media fashion, more than one in five registered voters let others know how they voted via social media.

Search

For most marketing professionals, the perception of search has long been one of an arcane and sometimes mysterious process defined by technical concepts like connectivity servers and link analysis; acronyms such as SEM (social engine marketing), SEO (search engine optimization), and SERP (search engine results page); and more menacing-sounding terms like "spiders" and "web crawlers." Search marketing means increasing traffic from search engines through greater optimization, and marketers are continually reminded of the myriad techniques—both sanctioned and forbidden—that might push their results to the top of the page.

Now, though, like almost everything else in the digital space, search must also adapt to the demands of social. In its quarterly survey of U.S. advertising agencies, media software company STRATA found that 69 percent of executives have made social the new focus of their digital ad spending, pushing it past search to second place behind display advertising.[19]

Social media is also playing a greater role in the business of search and is gradually replacing search engine optimization as the driving force. As Hirschhorn notes, social search is a variation of the process that takes into account the relationship among people when determining the results of queries, and factors in an array of social media sources:

> People don't really know, from a discovery perspective, everything they like. And social has been this wonderful thing that enables you to find a story, a thought, an image or a video that you didn't even know you were looking for. If you were asked if you were interested in that topic, you might likely say no. But because it has a social lens on it, because perhaps a friend who you have a lot of respect for, or someone you don't know but admire on Twitter, suggests something, that becomes a new means of discovery. So social has been very, very powerful in unearthing ideas and content that you didn't know you were looking for.

In addition to links and keywords to boost their brand's profiles, marketers must begin to think in terms of tweets, posts, "likes," and shares.

Google first warmed up to social media in 2010 when it decided to incorporate social components like author reputation, bookmarking, and commenting into its algorithm. Initially, it separated the results from its standard search format, but then decided to integrate them more seamlessly into its listings. By 2012, Google launched "Search, Plus Your World," which tracks down both content that has been shared only with Google+ members and matches from the public web. Not too long after, Microsoft rolled out its revamped Bing search engine, which went one step beyond Google by including users' contacts and activities on Facebook, Twitter, LinkedIn, Foursquare, and Google+.

The combination of search and social can be potent. Research by comScore and GroupM, a media investment management firm, has found that when a brand is exposed to consumers through both, its overall search clickthrough rates increase by more than 90 percent.[20] In addition, 40 percent of consumers whose purchase funnel includes search also use some form of social media to better inform their decisions.

Social search is still in its infancy, and channels like Facebook are developing their own search tools. The full effect of social media is still to been seen.

Vanishing Act

It has been said that most successful systems and technologies ultimately disappear. They become such a fixed part of life that they are eventually taken for granted. These days, there are still scores of books, blogs, online publications, and organizations dedicated to the advancement of social media. In time, though, they may no longer be needed, as people become as familiar and comfortable with social media as they have with every other medium that has preceded it.

Keep in Mind . . .

1. Nine out of 10 marketing professionals in the United States are using some form of social media, but many still lack the necessary knowledge or strategies to implement their programs effectively.
2. Worldwide, more than half of all corporate executives believe that social channels will enable their brands to better identify and

understand individual customers. For their part, though, consumers expect brands to listen and respond to their needs and interests before they will fully engage.

3. As brands recognize the growing importance of content in social strategies, a new breed of content marketers is taking on the kinds of responsibilities that have traditionally belonged to public relations professionals.

4. The number of crises that companies have been forced to deal with has grown steadily with the advent of social media, and these crises have occurred across all primary social channels.

5. Consumers increasingly get their news through channels such as YouTube and Twitter, which often break stories before conventional news organizations do.

6. While watching TV, more than half of all consumers with smartphones and tablets use them to share text messages, visit websites mentioned on shows, or verify information they have seen or heard during a program.

7. Candidates and elected officials alike increasingly rely on social media to get people to vote or get the word out around special issues.

8. Brands significantly improve their clickthrough rates when they are exposed to consumers through both search and social media.

9. Companies that apply social tools and strategies to their internal operations can improve productivity by as much as 25 percent.

Notes

1. "Social Media Usage Plateaus among Marketers," *eMarketer*, July 18, 2012, www.emarketer.com/Article.aspx?R=1009197.

2. IBM Institute for Business Value, "From Social Media to Social CRM: Reinventing the Customer Relationship," IBM, June 2011, http://public.dhe.ibm.com/common/ssi/ecm/en/gbe03416usen/GBE03416USEN.PDF.

3. Gartner, "Gartner Says Worldwide Social Media Revenue Forecast to Reach $16.9 Billion in 2012," July 25, 2012, www.gartner.com/it/page.jsp?id=2092217.

4. "For Brands, Social Media Shows Returns but Measurement Hurdles Remain," *eMarketer*, May 1, 2012, www.emarketer.com/Article.aspx?R=1009011.

5. Silverman Group and Unilever, "The Social Media Garden: A Digital Era Research Study of Social Media at Work," *SlideShare*, 2012, accessed September 4, 2012, www.slideshare.net/SMinOrgs/the-social-media-garden-report.

6. FedEx, "Corporations Transforming into Social Businesses, Says Second Study of Social Media Trends from FedEx and Ketchum," *FedEx Newsroom*, July 12, 2012, http://news.van.fedex.com/SocialBusinessStudy.

7. Nielsen Company, "Consumer Trust in Online, Social and Mobile Advertising Grows," *Nielsen Wire*, April 10, 2012, http://blog.nielsen.com/nielsenwire/media_entertainment/consumer-trust-in-online-social-and-mobile-advertising-grows/.

8. IBM, "Leading through Connections: Insights from the IBM Global CEO Study," 2012, accessed September 4, 2012, www-935.ibm.com/services/us/en/c-suite/ceostudy2012/.

9. Institute for Public Relations, "The Barcelona Declaration of Research Principles," June 18, 2010, www.instituteforpr.org/2010/06/the-barcelona-declaration-of-research-principles/.

10. International Association for the Measurement and Evaluation of Communication, "The March to Standards," *KDPaine's PR Measurement Blog*, June 15, 2012, http://kdpaine.blogs.com/files/smmstandards_markleinpaine_jun1512-1.

11. Gerard Corbett, "A Modern Definition of Public Relations," *Public Relations Defined*, March 1, 2012, http://prdefinition.prsa.org/index.php/2012/03/01/new-definition-of-public-relations/.

12. Jeremiah Owyang, "Social Media Crises on Rise: Be Prepared by Climbing the Social Business Hierarchy of Needs," *Web Strategy*, August 31, 2011, www.web-strategist.com/blog/2011/08/31/report-social-media-crises-on-rise-be-prepared-by-climbing-the-social-business-hierarchy-of-needs/.

13. Pew Research Center's Project for Excellence in Journalism, "A New Kind of Visual News," *Journalism.org*, July 16, 2012, www.journalism.org/analysis_report/youtube_news.

14. Amy Mitchell, Tom Rosenstiel, and Leah Christian, "What Facebook and Twitter Mean for News," *The State of the News Media 2012*, Pew Research Center's Project for Excellence in Journalism, http://stateofthemedia.org/2012/mobile-devices-and-news-consumption-some-good-signs-for-journalism/what-facebook-and-twitter-mean-for-news/?src=prc-section.

15. Aaron Smith and Jan Lauren Boyles, "The Rise of the 'Connected Viewer,' " *Pew Internet and American Life Project*, July 17, 2012, http://pewinternet.org/Reports/2012/Connected-viewers.aspx.

16. Simon Dumenco, "Social TV: An Astonishing 350 Million Posts and Check-Ins So Far This Year," *Ad Age*, July 13, 2012, http://adage.com/article/trending-topics/social-tv-350-million-interactions-year/236032/.

17. Sam Laird, "2012 Olympics: The Social Media Winners," *Mashable*, August 14, 2012, http://mashable.com/2012/08/14/2012-olympics-social-media-winners-infographic/.

18. Lee Rainie, "Social Media and Voting," *Pew Internet and American Life Project*, November 6, 2012, http://pewinternet.org/Reports/2012/Social-Vote-2012.aspx.

19. Joe Mandese, "Social Overtakes Search, Closes in on Display as Agencies' Top Digital Focus," *Online Media Daily*, May 3, 2012, www.mediapost.com/publications/article/173821/social-overtakes-search-closes-in-on-display-as-a.html.

20. Greg Sterling, "Search + Social Media Increases CTR by 94 Percent: Report," *Search Engine Land*, February 28, 2011, http://searchengineland.com/search-social-media-increases-ctr-by-94-percent-report-66231.

CHAPTER 3

Social Media Is a Complex System

C omplex systems are comprised of many distinctly autonomous yet interdependent parts, all of which interact in often unplanned and unpredictable ways. By that measure, just about every social, cultural, political, and economic institution is complex, as are the organizations within them. What is more, the larger a system gets, the more complicated it becomes. Perhaps it is nowhere more evident these days than in the realm of social media.

As an octopus, social media touches a variety of different business practices. As a complex system, it also pulls them together into myriad combinations so that individuals or entire divisions that once worked separately must now learn how to work together (Figure 3.1).

Largely driving this change is the consumer. Most consumers really don't care where information comes from, whether from marketing, public relations, or customer service. Nor does it matter if it is paid for, owned, or earned. What they are looking for is content that has real value in their lives and is available when and where they need it, in a form that is easy to access, understand, and use.

There is a general rule in technology that the easier a system is to use, the more intricate it is at the back end. Few people, for example, know how their TVs or telephones actually work. Even fewer need or want to know. The inner workings are hidden, and the user interface is relatively simple to operate. Such technologies are anything but transparent and probably shouldn't be. (This is changing somewhat with the advent of

Figure 3.1   The Brand Network

sophisticated smartphones and Internet TVs, but over time they, too, will likely hide more of their complexity if they hope to be as user friendly as their predecessors.)

The same principle applies to successful social strategies. The best of these strategies seamlessly integrates all their various elements, disguising the enormous complexity at the heart of them.

Who Owns Social?

Start with the numerous disciplines within an organization that may be responsible for social media initiatives. For the past several years, there have been occasional turf wars over the question of who owns social media. In most instances, marketing clearly exercises considerable control, but public relations, customer service, sales, product development, and information technology (IT) may also lay claim (Figure 3.2). The situation gets even more involved when outside agencies try to carve out their roles as well.

Then, of course, there is the ongoing confluence of paid, owned, and earned media, which now make up the lyric acronym POEM. Many marketers are taking their cues from audiences who care little about the different branches that create and distribute content, and they are merging the individual strengths of each channel in multiple socialized

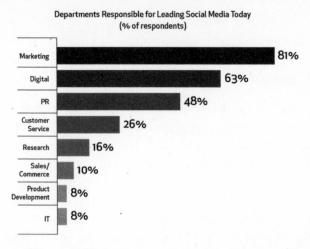

Departments Responsible for Leading Social Media Today
(% of respondents)

Figure 3.2   Today, Social Media Lives Primarily within Marketing, Digital, and PR

Source: Booz & Company/Buddy Media, "Campaigns to Capabilities: Social Media & Marketing 2011" Survey Results.

combinations. Although organizations may never completely demolish the silos that separate their sundry social media practitioners, they can learn to navigate them more effectively, but it will take more than occasionally crossing disciplinary borders to maximize the potential of converged media. Brands will ultimately have to reorganize their communication infrastructures and build new models for connecting with consumers.

So, no single discipline has a monopoly on social strategy because social media practices are softening the boundaries that separate traditional responsibilities. Instead, the real answer to the question of who owns social is that the consumers do, to the extent that they use it when, where, and how it suits their particular needs. In addition, even though marketing will still play a leading role in addressing the audience's interests and concerns, other parties will also bring their respective talents, resources, and agendas to the process.

The trick is for different departments to work together so that these sometimes divergent elements are indistinguishable, something that still does not come easily to many organizations. In a survey of more than 350 global marketing executives, IBM found that while most of them recognize the value of running social tactics as part of integrated

campaigns, barely one in five actually do so.[1] The rest do social media
discretely in silos and frequently on an ad hoc basis.

Cross Channels

Social strategy would be complex enough if the differences among
disciplines were the only complication, but social media outlets themselves exist as a collection of individual channels, each with its own purpose
and appeal. Some are designed for utility. Others are for playing games.
Still others function as places to post information, ideas, or images. Each
also plays by its own set of rules, and as hard as it may be for brands to
integrate campaigns internally, social networks are adding to the problem.

Indeed, even as companies attempt to take down barriers, some
networks appear to be creating new "walled gardens."[2] Both Facebook
and Twitter, for example, prevent Google from indexing their content,
thereby constructing barriers to Google+. Twitter also cut ties with
LinkedIn, Tumblr, and Instagram as part of an effort to restrict third-party
access to its network so that it can monetize its own resources.

Anywhere and Everywhere

Meanwhile, these changes are all happening across an expanding array of
media platforms, from those that fill an entire wall to others that fit in the
palm of a hand. More devices than ever are now nodes on the global
digital network, with still more to come. Gartner estimates that within
a year more than 6 billion devices will connect to the Internet.[3] This
growth should be of particular interest to marketers, as Gartner also
anticipates that before the end of the decade, chief marketing officers will
purchase more technology than chief information officers.[4]

It is no wonder, then, that marketing practitioners believe that
keeping pace with the growth of channels and devices will be their
number one challenge over the next three to five years.[5] Brands today
have to master an increasing array of technologies as consumers easily
traverse from one media platform to the next, sometimes using several
devices simultaneously. In fact, according to Google research, consumers
spend more than four hours of their daily leisure time in front of multiple
screens.[6] Earlier studies by the Altimeter Group suggest that consumers
can have as many as 75 variable encounters with channels, screens, and
content sources in the course of purchasing a product.[7]

To cope, as many as 90 percent of consumers multitask among technologies in various combinations that include TV, tablets, computers, and smartphones. Their ability to do so successfully may hinge on which devices they use, however.

A University of Texas at Austin study found that there is a correlation between levels of information overload and different media platforms.[8] Consumers of news on computers, e-readers such as the Kindle or NOOK, and Facebook are more prone to feel besieged by the amount of available content than those who rely on TV or smartphones. Readers of newspapers and magazines appear to be the least overwhelmed. The researchers suggest that the more isolated the experience—meaning fewer distractions—the less overload consumers feel. Accordingly, content in a magazine, on TV, or on a smartphone—all of which provide less room and opportunity for multiple media or links than do social media or websites on a desktop computer—are easier to digest.

A Holistic Approach to Social

Regardless of whether this line of research proves to be true over the long run, the sheer number of elements that make up social systems, along with the myriad explanations as to their effect, demonstrate just how complex social can be. Social media is clearly a complex system composed of multiple interacting components. At the same time, it is also part of an even larger scheme where it intersects with other systems like big data and cloud computing. Indeed, it is the ability to expeditiously collect and analyze massive amounts of information across a network of computers that contributes significantly to the value of social.

Understanding how each element works is integral to building effective social strategies, but knowing how they all work together is absolutely essential. Every successful strategy requires extensive knowledge of channels, devices, and consumers and their content preferences plus the context that is specific to each campaign. To that end, a holistic approach to marketing that recognizes how every part of the process interacts with and influences every other part is needed. Sometimes it is possible to bring down the silos, but more often it is a matter of proactively navigating among them. Whatever the approach, marketers today must be prepared to do it all.

Keep in Mind . . .

1. Within a single organization, social media can involve multiple disciplines, including marketing, public relations, customer service, sales, product development, and IT.
2. Social media also exists across an array of different channels, each with its own functions and characteristics.
3. Most marketers believe that keeping up with consumers as they easily move from one channel or platform to the next will be their number one challenge in the next three to five years.
4. The most effective way to meet that challenge will be to develop new and more comprehensive communication infrastructures and models for connecting with consumers.

Notes

1. IBM, "The State of Marketing 2012: IBM's Global Survey of Marketers," *SlideShare*, accessed September 4, 2012, www.slideshare.net/165yohodr/the-state-of-marketing-2012-ibms-global-survey-of-marketers-final.
2. As defined by Wikipedia: "A 'walled garden' refers to a closed or exclusive set of information services provided for users. This is in contrast to giving consumers unrestricted access to applications and content." June 13, 2012, http://en.wikipedia.org/wiki/Walled_garden_%28technology%29.
3. ExactTarget report featuring Gartner research, "Marketer's Guide to Multichannel Campaign Management," *Gartner Newsletter*, accessed September 4, 2012, www.gartner.com/technology/media-products/pdfindex.jsp?g=ExactTarget_issue1.
4. Freddie Laker and Hilding Anderson, "Five Challenges for Tomorrow's Global Leaders: Study," *Forbes*, August 21, 2012, www.forbes.com/sites/onmarketing/2012/08/21/five-challenges-for-tomorrows-global-marketing-leaders-study/.
5. IBM, "The State of Marketing 2012."
6. Google, "Navigating the New Multi-Screen World: Insights Show How Consumers Use Different Devices Together," *Google Mobile Ads Blog*, August 29, 2012, http://googlemobileads.blogspot.co.uk/2012/08/navigating-new-multi-screen-world.html.
7. Altimeter Group, "The Converged Media Imperative: How Brands Must Combine Paid, Owned, and Earned Media," *SlideShare*, July 19, 2012, www.slideshare.net/Altimeter/the-converged-media-imperative.
8. Avery E. Holton and Hsiang Iris Chyi, *Cyberpsychology, Behavior, and Social Networking* 15, no. 11 (November 2012): 619–624. doi:10.1089/cyber.2011.0610.

CHAPTER 4

The Brand Network

A s with almost any complex system, social media is a challenge to execute. It is comprised of myriad moving parts that are constantly changing and interacting. Accordingly, most social initiatives are made up of diverse and often distinctly different elements, so their outcomes may be unpredictable.

Brands can hardly afford to operate so erratically, though. They need a means to take all the fragmented pieces and pull them together to create cohesive and comprehensive strategies. Such continuity is at the core of effective social marketing. Despite the real-time nature of social media, however, for "always-on" to be "always great," there needs to be a better way to handle the complexity.

Think Like a Network

Until fairly recently, marketing was primarily the domain of traditional media. Even today, the bulk of advertising dollars still goes to TV, not just because the medium continues to reach the largest audience world-wide, but also because the considerable majority of consumers still believes that TV commercials are more effective than online advertising. Two-thirds (66 percent) of consumers surveyed by Adobe and research firm Edelman Berland say that the clout of TV spots outweighs that of web ads.[1] To this day, the majority (55 percent) prefers print advertising over what appears online.

Like publishers, TV executives have always understood their viewers and know how to create content that appeals to them. Television's top brass also know and understand something just as important: their brands.

In the realm of TV, a brand's network is composed of the various channels it owns and operates. In the early days (the 1950s through the 1970s), the brand consisted of a national broadcast network and a handful of local host stations. Throughout most of the United States, it meant no more than about a dozen touch points with viewers. With the growth of cable TV and its hundreds of available channels, however, came the need for networks to expand to keep pace with fragmenting audiences. The rise of the Internet has only made matters more complex.

For example, take Viacom, one of the world's leading media and entertainment brands. Its TV business alone consists of some of the most recognizable networks. Whether its programming is geared toward children (Nickelodeon), young adults (MTV), or men (Spike), each (and other channels) speaks to a specific audience, maintains a consistent voice, and delivers content within a regular format so that audiences know exactly what to expect.

The same is true of brands online. A brand's network is its collection of owned channels—from its website to its Facebook page to its YouTube channel and everything in between—all of which it uses to engage with and build audiences. In fact, the future direction of marketing is very similar to that of television; it is just shifting to encompass a host of different media. The notion of programming and channels readily transfers to the social world.

Consumers today have various channels through which they communicate with brands and with one another, and they can do so across multiple platforms. According to research from Google, American audiences spend most of their media time moving between their smartphones, tablets, computers, and TVs.[2] Where they land at any particular moment often depends on what is available, what they hope to achieve, and the amount of time needed. More and more, they also use their different devices simultaneously, which means that marketers must learn to appreciate, and even anticipate, consumers' changing preferences.

Indeed, a lot has been said about the need for brands to think of themselves as publishers, yet they also have to elevate their knowledge and skills to an even more strategic level. To drive scalable social media, brands must start to think of themselves not just as publishers, but also as networks.

Insight

Herb Scannell has worked in cable TV for more than 25 years. He began his career at Warner–Amex Satellite Entertainment and went on to become president of Nickelodeon and vice chairman of MTV Networks. Currently, he is president of BBC Worldwide America. He has also served as chairman and chief executive officer (CEO) of Next New Networks, a web TV company he cofounded in 2007 and which was subsequently acquired by YouTube.

I come from an MTV Networks background, where we were experts in understanding our audiences, and we did it through different vehicles. For example, at Nickelodeon we did more than 200 focus groups a year. We very much were aware of what's going on in kids' lives. We liked kids just the way they were—big, small, with teeth, without teeth. We were a kid-centric channel, and we wanted to know what was going on with them. And if we were really good at it, we reflected it in the on-air products that we made, including the promotion and packaging, which were oftentimes described as kind of cheeky or irreverent.

We did something similar when TNN split to Spike. The first thing we did was a study on what was going on in the lives of men. MTV was very much about youth culture and being on top of what was going on with teens and young adults. So the connection to consumers was primarily at that time through research, which was not just about validating shows; it was really about understanding the audience.

By the time I started Next New Networks, the equation had shifted, and though it was still about understanding the audience, now it was happening in real time, which meant continually listening to and connecting with audiences wherever they were. We were certainly part of the movement that said it wasn't important necessarily to be a destination like a website, but to be where the audiences were. So, we were supersyndicating our shows.

We had a concept at Next New Networks that saw the media world as a triangle. The top was broadcast, which was broad. The middle was cable, which was niche. And below that would be superniche, communities of people. If there were four to six broadcast channels, there'd be 50 to 150 cable channels, and then in the brave new world of the Internet

(*continued*)

(Continued)

there'd be 1,000 or 2,000 or 3,000 or [an] endless number of mininetworks—or "micronetworks," we called them at the time— that would be oriented toward special interests. That was the simplicity of the idea that we had, which is to go to where the audiences were.

We also knew that you couldn't just put stuff out there and magic would happen. We were also trying to make connections between the shows on this micronetwork by tapping into the network effect, which is to cross-promote against your many different offerings. And so we used the effect of having many verticals as a way to cross-pollinate. And at the end of the day, I think that is a big advantage.

Channel Architecture

Fundamental to the network model is the goal of advancing from the concept of brand as publisher to "brand as network," a network being a collection of multiple channels. Unlike in TV, however, where individual channels in the network are generally used to deliver specific messages to targeted audiences, the network model is built across a more integrated architecture that brings separate channels together in ways that create added value for the entire brand network.

Granted, every channel in a brand's network—whether it is YouTube, Twitter, or Facebook—is unique in its characteristics and function. For example, a company can put a video up on YouTube to demonstrate and highlight its product's features, whereas regular use of Twitter can support community development and customer service. So, understanding the personality and purpose of each channel is as important as knowing what content should go where. Doing so enables channel managers to determine the most effective time and place to post and allows them to apply the most appropriate metrics to gauge results. Moreover, identifying audience behavior within particular channels—and the etiquette that governs it—makes it that much easier to recognize what belongs on a channel and what does not.

It is also critical that channel architecture maps to a brand's overarching goals. Knowing how channels interact with one another is essential. A network's architecture likely includes its own website and blog along with the usual social suspects. The right operational framework not only supports these individual channels, but also delivers continuity across the network by cross-promoting and cross-colonizing them to help amplify whatever it is the brand wants to communicate. Thus, a healthy network is constantly active.

Conversation

How do you think about a brand's network so that each channel you are using serves a different purpose for the brand but ultimately drives the entire brand forward?

Mike McGraw, managing partner, Big Fuel: "When we come in and start a relationship with a brand partner, 9 out of 10 times we find that they are treating all of their channels the same way. All of the content is the same on all channels, and they are simply repurposing it without really thinking about the value that each of those channels can bring to the brand on an individual basis."

Stuart Schwartzapfel, vice president of audience insights, Big Fuel: "The notion of having channels and programming them like on television transfers very much to the social world. But instead of Fox or Bravo, you have YouTube, Facebook, and Twitter, and there is a brand that sits above and shapes the work and makes the content relevant to both that brand and its audience."

Andy Markowitz, director of global digital strategy, GE: "What we are doing at GE is employing many of our channels for multiple purposes. That includes influencers, enthusiasts, customers, consumers, the press. They are basically everywhere. So we focus on a number of different audiences, and we try to optimize channels based on where we think they are. But most people are in most places these days and we want to fish where the fish are, so to speak, so we find ourselves trying to satisfy a lot of those needs at the same time."

Rikard Steiber, global marketing director of mobile and social advertising, Google: "You have different touch points today. So if you have a brand that might have a following on Facebook, Twitter, Google+, LinkedIn, Pinterest, and so on, you might actually have a relationship with the same person

(continued)

(Continued)

across several different networks. You need to have some insights across these different platforms and make sure that you engage appropriately."

Sharon Feder, chief operating officer, Mashable: "I think it's important that when you're sharing content to channels you're not just sharing the same message across the board, or even thinking that the same content will carry through each channel, because different people use different channels for different things. They consume differently on those channels. For example, we know that something might perform very well on Facebook but do terribly on Google+. Or vice versa. And so we are thinking about what content plays best on what channel, what messaging plays best on what channel, and beyond that, how things are packaged."

Reggie Bradford, senior vice president of product development, Oracle: "I think it's a truly multichannel world. And as more and more consumers flock to social technologies, a Facebook strategy alone, or a Twitter strategy alone, is not going to get the job done. On the other hand, by invoking a multichannel approach, you get higher engagement on your baseline conversations. We have studies at Oracle that indicate that brands that use three or more social channels—and effectively harness the conversations across those channels—can get as much as 50 percent more engagement on their Facebook presence. For example, using your Facebook presence to create a Pinterest application or an Instagram application or a Spotify application garners more brand engagement."

The Grid

Keeping track of all that activity can be a monumental task unless there is a way to organize both the big and small elements, and that is at the heart of the grid. "Bottom line, it is about complexity and how best to manage it," says Christine Shoaf, managing director at Big Fuel. "That is why the network model works, because the grid is a simplified view, on a single page, of how it all comes together."

A grid is a system that is well-known to most TV audiences in the form of channel guides. Every cable system has at least one such guide, and they are also readily available on websites such as tvguide.com and zap2it.com. These easy-to-read visual lattices enable viewers to navigate the ever-expanding TV universe. They offer a simple way to identify what content is on what channel and when. What is more, they are thematic, not detailed, describing the essence of a show in just one or two sentences.

TV programmers are equally dependent on such grids to help them determine how to continually move viewers across their networks and keep them interested from one time slot to the next. Brands must also learn to apply this approach across the social landscape. To that end, the grid is a 12-month view of all network affairs and aligned with key milestones, such as large paid-media plans and special events (Figure 4.1).

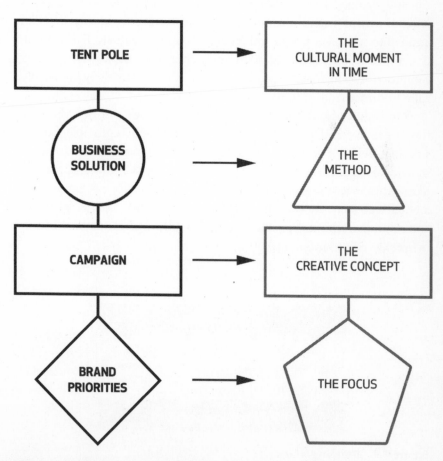

Figure 4.1   Programming the Network

Adds Shoaf, "You are programming against those occasions in ways that communicate the priorities of the brand to everybody who is involved, both internally and externally."

In addition to establishing and articulating priorities, a brand can use the grid to inform every facet of the network model, from the production and development of content to the editorial calendar. Just as important, every grid delineates how major paid-media investments can be leveraged to drive owned and earned media initiatives through the effective use of tent poles.

Grids are hardly static. They provide daily, weekly, monthly, and quarterly schedules for content delivery and management that sync with brand initiatives and messages. As the need for content changes, the grid can also change. Because the grid is created by a brand channel director, it relies on the brand channel management team to keep it regularly attuned to whatever people are relating to on its channels. Each channel director also works closely with researchers and strategists to closely monitor how audiences are shifting, which ensures that every bit of data is fully informed and optimized.

Grids differ from brand to brand, but the setup is always the same: timing, focus, and tent poles across the top, and repeatable business solutions below (Figure 4.2). It is important to note that grids do not list individual social media properties. Facebook, Twitter, Pinterest, and the like are places to house separate communities, but a network encompasses a brand's collectively owned audience. Grids identify messaging themes and solutions, whereas specific messages and their placement are laid out in weekly editorial calendars (Figure 4.3).

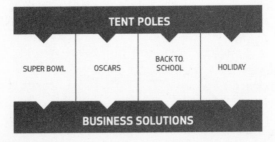

Figure 4.2   Building a Grid

Date	Day	Time	Platform	Content	Link	Assets	Char. Count	Status
10/		10:00	F	"Twitter ads are designed to be human - in a brand's 'voice,' but not robotic - and meld with the content around them." How do you think Twitter's ad platform stacks up against its competitors?	http://www.readwriteweb.com/archives/ads-arent-reshaping-twitter-twitter-is-reshaping-ads.php		193	Published
		10:00	T	Could an ad-free Facebook work? @JoshConstine explores the possibilities. [TECH] (via @TechCrunch)	http://tcrn.ch/QQrrG2		100	Published
		10:00	**T**	**Google+ could be back in the game if it conquers mobile http://tnw.co/Suxvr6 before Facebook does. [LINK] (via @chadcat @TNW)**			110	Published
		16:00	T	Or, as we like to say, "shareable." (via @JarrodorR2er) M1 http://bit.ly/SY6nJv0 @peretti 13 Ways To Make Something Go Viral [LINK]				
		10:00	F	Could Facebook influence age verification around the Web? Facebook recently made recommendations to the FTC regarding The Children's Online Privacy Protection Act. Read the full article on [TAG] InsideFacebook.com [LINK]	http://bit.ly/UD595P		221	Published
10/2/12	Tuesday	10:00	T	Google+ could be back in the game if it conquers mobile before Facebook does. [LINK] (via @chadcat @TNW)	http://tnw.co/Suxvr6		104	Published
		13:00	T	Today's critical reading: Where Facebook Is Looking to Grow, an interview with COO Sheryl Sandberg [LINK] (via @JBoorstin)	http://bit.ly/SXbRO2		122	Published
		16:00	T	What's your favorite #SocialTV app? Second Screen Experiences and Why They Work: [LINK] (via @socialmediaclub)	http://bit.ly/UDUbTw		110	Published
		10:00	F	LinkedIn debuted a new blogging platform yesterday that places the professional network square in the middle of the influence game. With its emphasis on quality content and engagement, do you think the follow feature is a good move for LinkedIn? Read the full article on [TAG] Fast Company: [LINK]	http://bit.ly/QAqIIs		297	Published
10/3/12	Wednesday	10:00	T	Why Facebook Users Like - and Unlike - brands: [LINK] (via @Janastas @marketingprofs) Which of these stats surprised you?	http://bit.ly/QKGrrX		121	Published
		13:00	T	Mining consumer data just got easier with @EricSchechter's Top 3 Tools for Listening to Social Chatter: [LINK] (@iMediaTweet)	http://bit.ly/Sw9SOl		125	Published

Figure 4.3 Big Fuel—Content Calendar

The power of the grid is also based on its capacity to expand its capabilities. Most grids are generally built around existing information and then incorporate additional insights to enhance their effect. For example:

- Annual or quarterly marketing plans that originate in the form of "product stories" that are intended to sell must be transformed into "people stories" designed to engage.
- Promotions, product launches, industry events, and other brand priorities that may not always be part of a marketing plan can be used to play a role in social.
- Historical successes, such as strategies and tactics that have worked in the recent past, can be applied.
- Newly emerging consumer activities and behavioral trends can be acknowledged and applied when and where appropriate.
- An existing media plan, or typical media behaviors, can be used to help identify the tent poles to which a brand or product is already aligned.

One of the best ways to better understand any complex system is to make it appear less complex. The grid does so by helping brands clearly visualize the network model.

Keep in Mind . . .

1. Despite the continued growth of online advertising, consumers still find TV and newspaper ads more compelling than ads in other media.
2. Like a TV network, a brand's network is a collection of its owned channels, including its website, blog, and various social channels.
3. The right channel architecture enables a brand to cross-promote its content to deliver continuity across its network and amplify its messages.
4. The grid is a yearlong view of all network activities—both large and small—aligned with key milestones.

Notes

1. Adobe, "Click Here: The State of Online Advertising," October 12, 2012, www
.adobe.com/aboutadobe/pressroom/pdfs/Adobe_State_of_Online_Advertising_
Study.

2. Google, "The New Multi-Screen World," August 2012, http://services.google
.com/fh/files/misc/multiscreenworld_final.pdf.

CHAPTER 5

Business Solutions

There are more than 500 TV channels in the United States. World-wide, the number reaches into the thousands. With 24 hours in a day, seven days a week, the math for TV programmers can be fairly over-whelming, yet it pales in comparison to the seemingly infinite amount of original content that one finds via the Internet.

Long ago, TV executives learned to deal with the challenge by developing content by genre—dramas, situation comedies, variety entertainment, news, sports, and, most recently, reality—and then programming them against specific parts of the day: daytime, prime-time, and late night. Since then, it has simply been a matter of continually coming up with new variations on these themes. For brands doing business online, there is a comparable method for keeping content flowing.

In the network model, business solutions are distinctive strategic initiatives designed to achieve long-term brand value. Like the various content categories that populate TV networks, they represent universal principles that can be applied throughout the social spectrum and can be used again and again because they always ring true with target audiences. Accordingly, they make it possible to globally standardize marketing strategies across channels and platforms.

"Whether a brand's goal is to increase its sales, expand the number of followers, respond to criticism, or improve sentiment, it can plug in the right business solution to achieve that," says Michoel Ogince, director of platform and product strategy at Big Fuel. The three-stage process requires asking the following right questions.

1. Business need analysis
   Does the brand need to:
   - Sell a product?
   - Grow its fan base?
   - Promote greater engagement with existing fans?
   - Win a share of conversation by creating authenticity or swaying sentiment?
   - Amplify paid media?
   - Move consumers down the sales funnel?
2. Organizing principle
   What is the best means to achieve any or all of the above?
   - What strategy will be implemented?
   - What creative content will be produced?
   - What social channels need to be leveraged?
   - Which vendors or platforms must be used?
   - What will be the key performance indicators (KPIs) that show ROI?
3. Solution offerings
   What is the correct combination of packaged offerings that is most suitable to fulfilling the business needs?

The answers, across a range of combinations, indicate the most appropriate business solution.

Social Commerce

Social commerce is a subset of electronic commerce through which social interactions contribute to selling and buying products online. Examples include user recommendations, customer reviews, brand communities, and social advertising. Although it is still a relative newcomer to the world of online transactions, Facebook's social commerce alone is expected to generate upward of $30 billion within the next few years.[1] By then, the research firm Gartner projects that companies will generate as much as half of all web sales via social or mobile media.[2]

Consumers are spending an increasing percentage of their time on social channels and relinquishing vast quantities of information about themselves. So, brands that can fully leverage social commerce and the personal data it amasses have a considerable advantage in the marketplace by being able to offer more relevant products and services.

Businesses can also realize value by effectively participating in consumer conversations. Here the goal is twofold. First, they can directly engage with targeted groups who have shown interest in, or expressed loyalty to, their brand to enhance relationships by providing access to exclusive deals, discounts, product updates, and product-related content. Second, brands can enable enthusiasts to promote them and potentially expand their customer base by facilitating connections between these fans and their friends.

Successful interactions with a brand's audience may not only result in better relations, but can possibly generate more satisfactory products and services as well. Research has shown that customers collectively innovate on a massive scale by adjusting or modifying products to better fit their needs.[3] The amount of money spent by American consumers to alter existing products, for example, is as much as one-third of what commercial enterprises invest in research and development. Thus, companies that can see their audiences not just as consumers but as "consumer-innovators" with whom they can engage have an added advantage.

So far, many brands treat social commerce as an extension of conventional e-commerce, even though social is a significant variation. "They are content to simply plant a shopping feature on Facebook or Twitter and wait for the money to roll in," says Big Fuel's Ogince. "But social demands its own strategy, one that recognizes consumers as an integral part of that strategy and encourages their participation at every point in the social marketing scheme."

Brandfluence

It has been said that great products sell themselves. Perhaps that is true, but in a world where vast amounts of data often overwhelm consumers, brands can use all the help they can get. So, marketers continually reach out to influencers in the social space, hoping to find the person or persons who can provide a surefire way to get an "in" anytime a brand seeks to align itself with a niche lifestyle segment.

Certainly, the influencer phenomenon is hardly new. Advertisers have relied on generations of celebrities to help move products and services. Still, many of today's social movers and shakers did not first make their names in movies, music, sports, or fashion; rather, they established themselves online. The Internet and social media have empowered "ordinary" individuals with specific interests or expertise to engage extraordinary numbers of people on a broad range of issues.

These casual thought leaders have been credited with shaping mass opinions—positively and negatively—by turning the spotlight on matters not normally touched on by traditional marketing or public relations and by increasing the value of earned and owned media.

Traditional media icons have also taken advantage of social media to boost their status. In the fall of 2012, pop star Lady Gaga became the first person to hit 30 million Twitter followers, beating out the likes of Justin Bieber and Katy Perry. Big numbers do not always translate into comparable clout, however, particularly when a growing percentage of tweets and likes are counterfeit and more apt to be initiated by robots than by real people. Nonetheless, when done correctly, "brandfluence" can help to substantially move the marketing needle.

Conversation

How can brands leverage their relationships with consumers to get advocates to literally speak on their behalf?

Jason Hirschhorn, owner, ReDEF Group: "The key is to identify who those influencers are and how you can create the dialogue, the understanding, and the proactive communication so that they understand where you are coming from and what your value proposition is."

Sharon Feder, chief operating officer, Mashable: "I think it is really important for all brands to view each consumer of their content and each person with whom they are interacting through social media as a potential brand influencer or advocate, and to establish long-term relationships that will help build their brands."

Stephanie Agresta, global director of social media and digital, MSL GROUP: "Digital influencers can help you keep your finger on the pulse of what's happening in social communities. And it's not just about 'listening campaigns' sometimes. Yes, you can definitely collect information through these channels, but by working more deeply with the people who are actually influencing those end users, you can stay ahead of the curve on what's popular. So there is a huge value in utilizing partners to amplify other marketing spending."

(continued)

(*Continued*)

Hirschhorn: "It's not something where you can buy them like you could buy a celebrity or a spokesperson. But if you have good content and they believe in it, they are going to be evangelists for you. And I think some of the interesting things happening in the technology space can help companies approximate where they should be spending their time. Not only in rudimentary ways like [using] keywords on Twitter and other things, but also by focusing on sentiment."

Agresta: "What is really interesting is that brands are not set up to think about influence in the context of their media buys, because their budgets come from different people. So there is a synergy that can be taken advantage of with regard to people who've built online communities and your own online community as a brand."

Using Google, Twitter, or third-party services like Twellow to identify influencers via keywords is time consuming and can prove difficult when applying filters to home in on geographic regions or determine particular numbers of followers. So, influencer identification platforms like Traackr and Appinions, which optimize the identification process, entered the market. Influencer platform SocMetrics, for example, lets users identify topical influencers according to their social footprint, influencer reach, and engagement metrics.

Once identified, cold-calling or pitching to an influencer is unlikely to create a connection because many of them prefer to work with marketers with whom they already have a relationship. Establishing such a bond can take weeks or even months. So, preparing long in advance is critical, although the initial contact can be something as simple as an introductory e-mail or tweet. Once that is done, keeping in touch via Facebook, Twitter, or LinkedIn should be mandatory.

Not all influencers are created equal, so knowing as much as possible about their social graphs and content preferences makes it a lot easier to tailor a campaign accordingly. Questions to ask include:

- What is their audience demographic?
- What type of content do their readers prefer: video, photos, text, or audio?

- Are there specific days, weeks, or months of the year when their content gets more views?
- Have they worked with other brands before? If so, have they been successful?
- How do they prefer to be reached: by phone, e-mail, text, Twitter, or direct message?
- Do they have colleagues who would be interested in working with the brand?

It is not unusual for influencers to be paid for their apparent power, either directly or through some form of incentive, but compensated content such as a blog post or review is often less than convincing. In fact, influencers engender a much smaller degree of consumer trust than do brand advocates, who do not require payment to endorse brands and their products because they are truly passionate about them.[4] Provenance may not be top of mind for audiences, but authenticity can count for a lot.

Finally, using spreadsheets to track influencer profiles and communication notes is labor-intensive and uneconomical. Social customer relationship management (CRM) systems improve workflow efficiency, data security, and the ability to scale. Platforms like Batchbook, Nimble, and CRM365 provide detailed social profiles, advanced search capabilities, cloud-based access, user permission levels, and communication logs.

SocialChorus is an influencer activation platform that makes it possible to automate content distribution at scale. The platform creates a branded microsite where influencers can log in and access content to share in their social streams. A rewards system encourages participation, and a real-time dashboard tracks influencer actions and statistics.

Although brands typically target influencers on well-established channels such as Facebook, Twitter, and YouTube, relative newcomers like Instagram and Pinterest are joining the playlist. There, brands can leverage the work of prominent photographers to shoot events or share their own content.

Advocacy

Connecting with an audience's passions is a proven way to build consumer relationships. Enabling them to promote those passions can result in new and even stronger relationships. Brand advocates are passionate about a brand or its products, so much so that, unlike influencers, they don't need incentives to share their affinities.

The number of people whom advocates can reach may be considerably smaller than that of most influencers, but they still create more than twice as many brand-related communications as the average web user. Moreover, the level of trust they inspire can be appreciably greater because they are regarded as being more authentic. They are also 70 percent more likely than other users to be considered a valuable source of information and 50 percent more prone to post material that influences a purchase.[5]

To their credit, advocates are prolific creators of information, and brands need to provide them with the tools and opportunities to keep it flowing. As with influencers, the first step is to leverage technology so as to identify the best among them. Consumer-to-consumer platforms such as Booshaka and FanGager enable brands to exploit the power of word-of-mouth marketing.

A brand's advocate population can then be amplified to include a much larger set of consumers in the following ways:

- By allowing advocates to customize default sharing options in e-mails, Facebook, Twitter, Google+, and the like, making it easy to converse about the brand's products and services
- By giving advocates added incentives, such as discounts, loyalty points, gift cards, and charitable donations, along with similar offers to friends with whom they connect, thus increasing participation
- By capitalizing on the human impulse to compete, excel, and be recognized for achievement through various forms of recognition

To that end, companies like Extole and Zuberance are turning one-directional marketing on its head by tapping in to the power of customer advocates to foster trusted word-of-mouth stories about a brand.

User-Generated Content

Like influencers, user-generated content (UGC) is not entirely new. Some of the most important events occurring at the end of the twentieth century—the fall of the Berlin Wall (1989), the San Francisco earthquake

(1989), and the Rodney King beating (1991)—were captured by ordinary folks with video cameras. At the time, TV news departments cautiously welcomed the birth of citizen journalism by inviting viewers to submit taped stories, but firmly controlled whether the images would be seen by large audiences. But with the advent of the Internet, cell phone cameras, and social media, all of that has changed.

Although they may not have millions, thousands, or even hundreds of friends or followers, individual web users can still influence events with a well-timed tweet or Facebook post. Consider, for example, the hidden video camera that caught Mitt Romney as he apparently dismissed nearly half the American electorate during a fund-raising event. The 69-second clip helped neutralize tens of millions of dollars of paid political advertising.

Today, 25 percent of search results for the 20 largest global brands are links to UGC.[6] That is why chief marketing officers and their ilk—like news directors a generation ago—are integrating UGC into the content mix.

This approach has several advantages. First, the cost—as with so many other things digital—is minimal compared to the price tag for most professionally produced content, and the quality of cell phone cameras is far superior to that of the consumer devices that recorded history more than two decades ago. Second, audiences are quite comfortable with content produced by their peers. According to a study from Boston University, over the past four years, consumer-generated ads have earned the best ratings in the Kellogg School of Management Super Bowl Advertising Review.[7] They have also ranked at the top of *USA Today*'s Ad Meter and have generated the most buzz for brands. In addition, brands are glad to solicit material from consumers to supplement their own content, driving down production costs while driving up social engagement.

Of course, not all types of consumer content are solicited or even welcomed, as is seen by the myriad examples of angry customers who have taken their complaints to the web. Too many companies still lack the proper programs, staff, and policies to address such problems effectively.[8] Worse, perhaps, is that some brands attempt to strike back at consumers whom they believe have wronged them. Several small businesses have begun to sue former customers for posting negative reviews on sites like Yelp. Federal law prevents companies from going after the websites, but complainants are fair game. Of course, businesses risk even more damaging consumer backlash if they choose to fight back.

Brands are better served when they understand what impels social media content and what effect they actually may have. Research of online comments and reviews on 200 different products found, not surprisingly, that customers who have strong opinions are the most willing to post comments.[9] Many, however, tend to skew negatively simply to stand out from the crowd. Over time, the comments tend to become even more negative because the most involved reviewers begin to dominate the forum and push less engaged participants to the sidelines. Consequently, although most consumers may hold a brand in good standing, they may at times comprise a silent majority.

Gaming

Social gaming uses the principles of game design, game thinking, and game mechanics, all of which are becoming popular marketing techniques. Findings from Oracle's Social Marketing Cloud Service show that the launch of a new game can increase brand engagement tenfold, with three out of every four users coming back for more.[10] In addition, introducing a new game on a site like Facebook can reduce a brand's average "cost per 'like'" by as much as 60 percent. Such outcomes have led Gartner to predict that more than 70 percent of Global 2000 organizations will have at least one gamified application by 2014,[11] with player growth moving across multiple platforms.[12]

To create brand awareness and drive user engagement such as comments, shares, and retweets, games must provide opportunities for achievement, often through the use of points to reward consumers for their participation. Gifts are another type of offering that games use to motivate users. Although some games use real-world gifts in the form of money or gift cards, others motivate players with virtual gifts. Foursquare's badges are an example of this technique.

At the same time, games must expose users to a variety of emotional experiences, including the following:

- Clear goals
- A high degree of concentration
- A loss of self-consciousness

- Direct and immediate feedback
- Balance between ability level and challenge
- Personal control over the situation or activity
- Total absorption in the activity
- An intrinsic sense of reward

Of course, the appearance of leader boards displaying the names of the highest scorers also helps to feed the competitive spirit.

Those common properties apply to almost all forms of social gaming. A study by Stefanie Hermann of Reutlingen University in Germany found that a successful game challenge must nonetheless be tailor-made to address its individual target audience, its business objective, and the underlying application of the game itself.[13] Otherwise, users will quickly tire of a one-size-fits-all approach.

Paid Social

In the realm of conventional advertising, not just any content has been king; paid content has ruled, until fairly recently. The rise of social media has brought with it new attention to the value of owned and earned media, but the focus is changing once more.

Market saturation, channel competition, the battle over consumers' diminishing attention spans, and earned media—by nature of its organic distribution—being notoriously hard to target are all reasons for these shifts. Currently, however, all those reasons, either individually or in aggregate, decrease social return on investment. So, marketers are learning to bring paid media back into the fold alongside their owned and earned strategies to harness the broadest possible reach and engagement.

Research by Facebook and comScore has shown that companies adding paid media to the top 100 Facebook pages were able to garner more than five times the number of "likes" from users.[14] What is more, of three brands studied—a telecommunications company, a major retailer, and a financial services firm—each was able to use paid media to extend its reach 500 percent in a single week. Most important, those users who were reached through paid media were more likely than the average Facebook user to purchase a product or service.

Such results can be achieved through two specific methods of using paid media to enhance social marketing efforts. One way is as a conversation catalyst. Brands can leverage tools like promoted tweets and trends to accelerate social conversation, especially around big tent-pole events like the Super Bowl. The other is to use paid media as a growth engine for social applications. Many brands have taken this approach to grow their numbers of followers and fans by expanding promoted tweets to existing followers through search results, promoted trends, and promoted accounts.

Brands can make sure that their audiences see all that positive social coverage by adopting integrated strategies that combine the best of earned and paid media in a social context, using paid media to target specific interest verticals, demographics, and geographies. Several steps are involved:

- Acquisition: driving traffic to owned channels and optimizing conversion rates
- Retention: targeting media against new users and driving them back to owned channels while keeping current users engaged
- Persistent communication: implementing an always-on strategy to keep media persistent and channel new content to new and current users

Additional best practices include placing ad dollars in one or multiple buckets, such as:

- Twitter: promoted tweets, accounts, and trends
- Facebook: Facebook ads and marketplace ads
- Video distribution
- In-game advertising

Keep in Mind . . .

1. Business solutions are repeatable social media applications that are relevant and true for any brand, regardless of what it makes or sells.
2. Although social commerce is a subset of electronic commerce, it requires a unique strategy that leverages interactions with

consumers—and the data these interactions produce—to enhance sales efforts.

3. Influencers often expect some form of payment or other incentives to promote a brand, whereas advocates are so passionate about a brand or its products that they don't require incentives.

4. User-generated content can have a significant impact—positive or negative—on a brand, so it is imperative that companies understand what compels consumers to express their opinions online.

5. For games to generate brand awareness and drive user engagement, they must target users' emotions and provide opportunities for achievement.

6. Research has shown that incorporating paid media into social engagements can significantly extend a brand's reach and increase the possibility that consumers will purchase its products or services.

Notes

1. "F-Commerce Will Reach $30 Billion in 2015 as Reported in Recent Facebook Social Commerce Trends Study," *PRWeb*, April 3, 2012, www.prweb.com/releases/facebook-social-commerce/f-commerce/prweb9337545.htm.

2. Jackie Cohen, "Facebook Will Be 50% of Online Retail by 2015: Infographic," *All Facebook*, November 7, 2011, http://allfacebook.com/facebook-commerce-201_b65830.

3. Eric von Hippel, Susumu Ogawa, and Jeroen P. J. de Jong, "The Age of Consumer-Innovator," *MIT Sloan Management Review*, September 21, 2011, http://sloanreview.mit.edu/the-magazine/2011-fall/53105/the-age-of-the-consumer-innovator/.

4. "Influencers vs. Brand Advocates," Visual.ly, accessed October 4, 2012, http://visual.ly/influencers-vs-brand-advocates.

5. "Field Guide to Brand Advocates," BzzAgent, accessed October 4, 2012, http://about.bzzagent.com/word-of-mouth/go/field-guide.

6. Chris Aarons, Andru Edwards, and Xavier Lanier, "Turning Blogs and User-Generated Content into Search Engine Results," *ClickZ Stats SES Magazine*, June 8, 2011.

7. Benjamin Lawrence, Susan Fournier and Frederic Brunel, "When Companies Don't Make the Ad: A Multi-Method Inquiry into the Differential Effectiveness of Consumer-Generated Advertising," Boston University School of Management Research Paper No. 2012-29, *Social Science Research Network*, October 18, 2012, http://papers.ssrn.com/sol3/papers.cfm?abstract_id=2166657.

8. Erica Swallow, "The Anatomy of a Social Media Crisis," *Mashable*, August 31, 2011, http://mashable.com/2011/08/31/social-media-crisis/.

9. Wendy Moe, David A. Schweidel, and Michael Trusov, "What Influences Customers' Online Comments," *MIT Sloan Management Review*, September 21, 2011, http://sloanreview.mit.edu/the-magazine/2011-fall/53102/what-influences-customers-online-comments/.

10. Oracle White Paper, "Using Social Gaming to Drive Engagement: Insights and Best Practices for Brand Managers," August 2012, www.oracle.com/us/products/social-gaming-for-engagement-1841595.pdf.

11. Gartner, Inc., "Gartner Predicts Over 70 Percent of Global 2000 Organizations Will Have at Least One Gamified Application by 2014," November 9, 2011, www.gartner.com/it/page.jsp?id=1844115.

12. The Nielsen Company, "U.S. Gaming: A 360° View," February 7, 2012, www.nielsen.com/content/dam/corporate/us/en/reports-downloads/2012-Webinars/US-Gaming-A-360-View.pdf.

13. Ivan Kuo, "Research in Gamification Theory and Factors of Success," Gamification Corporation, January 25, 2012, www.gamification.co/2012/01/25/research-in-gamification-theory-and-factors-of-success/.

14. David Cohen, "Facebook, comScore Study Touts Benefits of Paid Media, Even for Larger Brands," *AllFacebook*, October 24, 2012, http://allfacebook.com/understanding-paid-and-earned-reach-on-facebook_b102952.

The Value of the Network

CHAPTER 6

Higher Highs and Higher Lows

The differences between the strategies underlying social marketing and those that direct both traditional and digital advertising are considerable. Advertising is fundamentally a one-way communication, whereas social marketing relies on listening as well as talking. Advertisers are most comfortable when they control all aspects of the message. Social marketers are, at the very least, learning to let go of such control. Perhaps the most important distinction is that advertising tends to focus on short-term objectives and one-off campaigns, whereas growing a successful brand network is a long-term commitment.

In a world where information is overabundant and attention hard to come by, thinking long term—and getting others to do so—is a challenge. As noted in Chapter 1, American consumers are exposed to as many as 3,000 forms of advertising every single day. Over the course of a year, that amounts to more than 1 million marketing messages, all of which compete to get noticed, not just with one another, but with innumerable other forms of content as well. How, then, does a brand start, build, and sustain relationships with consumers?

Paid, Owned, and Earned Media

When brands spend money, they get awareness. Logically speaking, higher spends result in higher levels of awareness. That is the paid-media flow. Joint research out of the University of Pittsburgh and Carnegie Mellon University has shown that where owned and earned media are efficient ways to foster existing relationships with consumers, paid media is more effective at *initiating* them.[1] According to the findings, on a per-event basis, promotions from traditional media sources can generate nearly 10 times the amount of sales from new customers than either a blog post or a mention in an online community. They can also muster from 5 to 10 times the number of repeat sales. (See Figure I.1 Traditional Media and Promotional Flow on page 5.)

The problem arises when brands stop spending money because that is when attrition begins, but it is also the time to leverage earned and owned media. As the University of Pittsburgh/Carnegie Mellon University study points out, because these forms of content appear far more frequently in the span of a social campaign than their paid counterparts, they have a significantly greater effect over time. Thus, the primary role of owned and earned media within the network model is to drive the highs higher where the campaign peaks while keeping the lows as elevated as possible at points in between. (See Figure I.2 Higher Highs and Higher Lows on page 5.)

Insight

As president of BBC Worldwide America, Herb Scannell is responsible for growing the BBC brand and the business across all divisions in the United States.

When I hired the guy who is running the on-air promotion group for BBC America, he said, "I can reach a lot of people with a clever on-air promo spot that I make with my left hand; but with my right hand, I can reach more people by being really smart and savvy about how I connect to audiences with social media." So this right-hand/left-hand combination is what we have got to be using. We just can't do what we used to do back in the 1990s. This is the kind of thinking that somebody has to have when they are a marketing person. They have to think about the combination of the different tools they have.

Extending the Life Span of Content

For years, scientists and marketers alike have assumed that the working memory for most people—the amount of information that their brains can consciously hold at any given moment—is capable of remembering somewhere around seven different ideas at the same time. Recent research, however, suggests that this assumption may be too generous, and that working memory may actually have a maximum capacity of just three or four concepts.[2] To make matters worse, people generally forget 90 percent of a presentation within 30 days, and most of that happens within the first few hours.[3]

Still, there are several effective concepts that social marketers should focus on when trying to increase the life span of people's memories and thus maintain their attention. For example, information is best remembered when it is meaningful and contextual[4]—when it touches someone's passion points. Events that arouse emotions are remembered longer, and can be called up more easily, than those that are neutral.

It is also effective to reiterate and reinforce content at timed intervals. Such repetition is critical because memory is enhanced when people can associate a message with something they have seen or heard before. Regularly adding to a person's knowledge base each time the original material is repeated also captures attention and boosts memory. Plus, learning improves when new information is introduced over time.

Taking the time and effort to create a comprehensive content strategy can pay off. Information that is carefully thought out, organized, and constructed is considerably more likely to be well received and remembered than thrown-together attempts.

All these principles help the network model and advance its capacity in several ways:

- By driving amplification around major tent poles or key initiatives
- By maintaining continuity by connecting the dots from campaign to campaign
- By establishing an operational foundation with the right talent, tools, and processes

These strategies are necessary to the long-term values of a brand network. Highs and the lows continue to climb higher and higher, creating a long-term "network effect." (See Figure I.4 on page 8.)

Keep in Mind . . .

1. Traditional advertising strategies focus on short-term objectives, whereas applying the network model is a long-term commitment.
2. Paid media is generally more effective at creating new relationships with consumers, whereas owned and earned media are crucial to extending and sustaining those relationships.
3. New information is best remembered when it is meaningful and reinforced over time.

Notes

1. Andrew T. Stephen and Jeff Galak, "The Complementary Roles of Traditional and Social Media in Driving Marketing Performance," Insead, accessed October 10, 2012, http://bear.warrington.ufl.edu/weitz/mar7786/Articles/social%20and%20tradiitonal%20media.pdf.
2. David Rock, *Your Brain at Work* (New York: HarperBusiness, 2009), 21.
3. John Medina, *Brain Rules* (Seattle: Pear Press, 2008), 100.
4. Ibid., 114.

CHAPTER 7

Amplification

In the early 1980s, the Fabergé cosmetics brand produced a now-celebrated television commercial for its "Organics" shampoo in which the spokesperson urged viewers, "If you tell two friends about Fabergé Organics Shampoo with wheat germ oil and honey, then they will tell two friends, and so on and so on and so on."[1] Although it is probably not the first example of viral marketing, this classic piece of paid media is certainly one of the best remembered. Fast-forward some 30 years later, and it is mentioned on more than two dozen websites and has several uploads on YouTube, making it a prime example of a well-amplified brand.

These days, of course, the process of crossing marketing channels can occur almost instantly. In fact, when discussing their strategies, marketers increasingly refer to paid, owned, and earned media in the same breath. Word-of-mouth back in the 1980s was literally that, requiring participants to actually talk to each other, but now, like just about everything else, it is far more complex. Brands are forced to evaluate the relationship between channels, platforms, media, and audiences with each new social campaign.

Tent Poles

If the grid is the basis for building long-term relationships with consumers, tent poles are the repeatedly occurring inflection points that keep the relationships interesting. They are cultural landmark moments that drive consumers to discuss relevant and related issues online. They may be one-off instances or perennial occurrences, but the most successful of them engender ongoing conversations. Among the best known tent poles in the United States are the Super Bowl and Olympics sporting events, the Oscar and Grammy awards shows, and such as the Harry Potter and Batman films and entertainment franchises.

For a giant brand like General Motors, classic tent poles include the Olympics, Super Bowl, and Oscars. Brands hope that every multimillion-dollar ad broadcast during one of these events is a critical focal point at a given moment in time. They need not rely solely on the effect provided by big-ticket events, however. Important internal milestones, such as new product launches, can also draw considerable attention.

After more than a year of positioning its spokesperson, Carly Foulkes, in magenta summer dresses and enveloped by white surroundings, T-Mobile abruptly inaugurated a rebranded ad campaign, featuring Foulkes attired in black and pink leather biker gear atop a Ducati motorcycle, set against a dark background. In the company's blog, this dramatic departure was described by senior vice president Peter DeLuca as "a metaphor for what T-Mobile is all about—challenging the status quo and taking bold steps in the marketplace as a challenger brand."[2] It resonated with audiences and was the first in a series of ads promoting T-Mobile's product relaunch.

Insight

When Herb Scannell cofounded Next New Networks, his goal was to build a series of Internet television networks targeted to niche communities where viewers could contribute and share content.

At Next New Networks we would hold programming meetings, and we would be very conscious of the fact that the Internet is a very "now" medium. We always knew when things were going to happen that would reflect the pop culture—whether it was holidays—which are obvious—or releases of big movies, things that were happening on television or important birth dates. We were very thoughtful about programming, and every one of the verticals had a charge to figure out what events they wanted to champion and what they would be doing for it.

Extending Conversations

Although the types of tent poles may differ from industry to industry, and even within companies themselves, they align paid media with the kinds of owned and earned media that propel social conversations. Another way to envision them is as the towers that support a suspension bridge (Figure 7.1). Along with the suspension cables that run between them, these towers carry the weight of the deck below, where the traffic crosses. In much the same way, a brand's tent poles support the grid, and various business solutions fuel the conversations that move across it.

Usually, a grid needs at least four tent poles to sustain interest over an extended period. In the 2012 presidential election, for example, tent poles included the primary debates (which themselves contained quite a number of poles), the national conventions, the presidential candidates' debates, and finally the election itself.

Not all tent poles are of this scale, however. Sometimes it is necessary to take advantage of more limited opportunities, such as incorporating poles that accentuate conversations among smaller communities or around niche topics, both of which can be aligned to programs that are still part of a brand's media budget. For example, in addition to spending big on major media events, General Motors also takes advantage of annual auto shows in cities across the country.

Nor must brands rely on multiple tent poles to make an impression. For a company such as 1-800-FLOWERS, Valentine's Day and Mother's

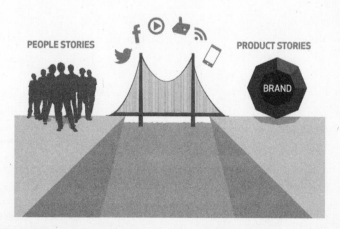

Figure 7.1   Connecting People Stories to Product Stories

Insight

As Nestlé's global head of digital and social media, Pete Blackshaw is responsible for staying on top of issues and managing how they appear in social media conversations.

One of the best examples of idea amplification at Nestlé is our Contrex water brand in France, where their big idea is that slimming can be fun. They do a decent amount of television, but they also produced a separate piece of video content around this notion of swimming being fun that they got on air ahead of the actual TV buy, and then built a massive conversation around it. I think it is actually one of the most successful YouTube videos in Europe, and it primed the TV element. They kept nurturing the conversation across multiple platforms and listened intently to what was being said, and dialed it up whenever they could. So this is a good example of where a big idea actually found a lot of incremental life in the social and digital environment.

Insight

Andy Markowitz, director of global digital strategy at GE, leads a global unit in driving stakeholder connections and conversations across the entire organization, including social media content and customer engagement.

There are about four times a year when we can actually see a customer in person—at their office twice a year, and at a trade show once or twice a year. So what we try to do with our communities is to fill the gap between the instances when we see them. One of the ways we do that is [with] something called Access GE, which is a platform for GE Capital's midmarket financial customers. If you're a customer, you can go in and participate in any number of discussions, whether it's around finance or human resources or general business strategy.

> *We also bring in content from a number of different sources, such as McKinsey, which we pay for, or [content] that our customers get access to.*
>
> *If you come in and you have a question about lean manufacturing, somewhere in GE we have plenty of experts on lean manufacturing. If you want to talk to someone about how to do digital marketing, we have experts on that, too. Essentially, Access GE is about access to information that you really can't get anywhere else. And we have taken a very advanced step in putting together something that leverages social as a differentiator and a competitive advantage.*

Day are the peak times of the year. For a retailer like the Children's Place, the one major tent pole is its back-to-school campaign because the majority of its sales come at that time of the year.

In every case, however, the more relevant the tent poles are and the more they can drive emotional responses, the greater the chance of success in promoting socially shared content. Brands are adopting this mind-set as they shift from advertising-focused messages to content- and conversation-focused marketing, and this model is relevant not just to social media, but to marketing overall.

Keep in Mind . . .

1. Tent poles are strategically placed events that help brands reach high points of awareness throughout a long campaign.
2. Tent poles can be created internally around product launches and refreshes, or they can be linked to big outside events and cultural milestones.
3. Although most brands rely on at least four or more major tent poles over the course of a campaign, they can effectively leverage fewer and smaller inflection points if they are relevant and compelling to consumers.

Notes

1. "Fabergé Shampoo," YouTube, December 29, 2007, www.youtube.com/watch ?v=TgDxWNV4wWY.

2. Peter DeLuca, "T-Mobile's 'Alter Ego,'" *T-Mobile Issues and Insights Blog*, April 17, 2012, http://blog.t-mobile.com/2012/04/17/t-mobile%E2%80%99s-alter-ego/.

CHAPTER 8

Continuity

I f great content is the spark that ignites audience engagement, absorbing conversation is the fuel that sustains it. So, it is no wonder that channel and community management are the most common roles within social media.[1] Content teams are tasked with creating compelling content, but it is the management teams that are responsible for nurturing it and ensuring that it is consistent across all channels and communities.

As noted in Chapter 4, a brand's network is similar to that of TV. Both are composed of the various channels they own and operate, whether it is Viacom's MTV or any brand's Facebook pages. There the similarity ends, however, because a critical component of most social channels is the communities that reside there.

Insight

As Big Fuel's vice president of brand channel management, Mandy Gresh oversees the firm's channel and community managers.

The dictionary defines a community as "a social group of any size whose members reside in a specific locality, share government, and often have a common cultural and historical heritage."
So, in social media one could say:

- The locality is the channel—such as Facebook or YouTube— where the community lives.

(continued)

(*Continued*)

- The government is the community guidelines set up to moderate the conversations (for harsh language, etc.).
- The common cultural and historical heritage is the affinity for a brand and/or what it says about community members and their interests.

Essentially, when people "like" a brand on Facebook, follow it on Twitter, or tag it in a photo on Instagram, it is because it means something in their lives. They may be saying that they love the brand; or more likely, they love what being affiliated with that brand says about them.

Inevitably, a social community is a place where people share their own brand-related stories and/or seek out others' stories. Building an active and engaged community means having people who are always "on" for a brand and, in a sense, become its day-to-day bread and butter.

Vibrant communities are at the heart of the most successful channels; and at the root of Brand Channel Management is the channel architecture. As part of the network model, the channel architecture provides the who, what, where, when, why, and how of each social channel.

Channel Architecture

Social channels do not simply support a brand. They also support one another. Understanding how channels work and how users engage with them is a prerequisite for making strategic decisions about where to place content to achieve the best results.

Crucial to the network model is the architecture that provides the operational framework for each social channel. Every channel serves a specific purpose, delivering content to a specific audience. For example, half of all social media users are between 25 and 44 years old, but the age distribution varies widely.[2] Tumblr and reddit are among the "youngest" networks, with half or more of their users being under age 35. At the other end of the spectrum, LinkedIn is the "oldest" network, with 79 percent of users age 35 and older. In the middle are Twitter and Facebook, with 55 percent and 65 percent, respectively, age 35 and older.

Disparities in how users experience each channel also are important indicators. In its study of how emotions differ between personal and professional networks, LinkedIn found that users' priorities on personal channels include staying in touch, being entertained, killing time, and sharing their own content.[3] Time spent on professional sites, on the other hand, is often driven by the desire for self-improvement, whether by searching for new opportunities, establishing useful contacts, maintaining professional identities, or keeping careers up to date. Not surprisingly, users on both types of networks expect content to conform with their objectives.

Different businesses also have separate agendas. There are major governance issues surrounding what can be said about the safety of drugs or the performance of automobiles. Other heavily regulated industries like health care, insurance, and financial services must deal with similar restraints. Entertainment companies, hotels, and most consumer goods brands have more opportunities to tell stories, present images, or be funny. In general, the more conservative a brand is required to be, the more restricted its social posture.

Finally, a consummate understanding of channel architecture also includes the platforms by which members connect to their various communities. Google's research into the matter found that computers are principally used to find information, whereas tablets primarily provide entertainment.[4] For their part, the ubiquity and portability of smart-phones make them ideal for staying connected.

By looking at every channel individually, identifying tone and personality, applying metrics to each, and even breaking out time of day, brands can optimize channels both separately and as parts of a more complex network model. Just as publishers intrinsically know what does and does not work for a particular magazine, proper channel architecture offers brands insights on how best to use each channel, helping them understand what kind of content to post and when, and what kinds of responses to look for.

Conversation

How does channel management help brands connect the dots between paid media campaigns and enable them to stay relevant?

(continued)

(Continued)

Sharon Feder, chief operating officer, Mashable: "There are two different goals here. One is engaging the community you already have; and the second is really community acquisition, which is bringing new community members into the fold."

Pete Blackshaw, global head of digital and social media, Nestlé: "I think this is where platforms like Facebook and Twitter become so incredibly important, because independent of the campaigns, consumers still want to engage."

Jason Hirschhorn, owner, ReDEF Group: "There's a lot of talk about storytelling. And certainly this is not new to a brand. But now it has to be a continuous story. Not just the one commercial that you put out there, because people are inundated with information from all different places. What's more, they're into one platform over others at any given point of time. And there are different levels of engagement for a brand. So you have to think about all the brand touch points and how you tell a story."

Ted Rubin, chief social marketing officer, Collective Bias: "Think about it as just normal friendships, but being able to do it at scale so that you can create conversations about your business that go on even when you aren't spending marketing dollars. You can create brand advocates who have real knowledge and insight, and feel like they are a part of your business because they are getting information from you on a regular basis."

Feder: "Being on these communities, being on these platforms, and seeing how a particular community interacts with you on a regular basis really provides a brand an opportunity to understand what kind of content, what kind of formats, what kind of topics work best."

Blackshaw: "So publishing has to have a steady consistency. Across all of our brands at Nestlé, there's a real consistency in publishing, whether it's two or three posts a day or, if there's a heavy up in TV, even more activity. But I definitely see social media as an opportunity to maintain consistency throughout."

Brand Channel Management

Within the network model, there is typically a channel manager and a community manager who work with the brand to develop and implement a unique channel architecture, containing a set of guidelines for each channel (Figure 8.1). These codes of behavior help define a brand's social mission and the substance of its content. In addition, they identify both the primary audience (those consumers the brand is directly targeting) along with any peripheral individuals or groups who may influence perceptions and opinions.

Because some brands are still uncertain about why they are using social media, channel management often begins with the following questions:

- Who is the channel audience, and what types of content do they engage with?
- When will they use each channel?
- What are other competitive brands doing? What is working for them and what is not?
- Why should the brand be (or not be) on this particular channel?

Channel	Mission	Tone	Content (for guideline purposes only)
Facebook	The largest of the mass social channels. The central social loyalty platform.	Conversational, engaging, questions, polls.	All content types, mass channel.
Twitter	A fast-paced stream of what's happening right now. Users tend to gravitate to topics first and individuals secondarily.	Direct and without embellishment.	140 text characters. Links to external content.

Figure 8.1   Channel Architecture Excerpt

- How can the brand leverage each relevant channel for content sharing and planning?

The answers to these questions are then translated into a brand's channel architecture, providing the appropriate cadence for its mission, tone, content, and audience with respect to each social channel.

Sometimes it is helpful to divide channel management into two strategic stages. The first is a campaign-driven strategy, whereby a brand can market a product by building the campaign and determining how it will live in the channel. At that point, it is necessary to continually manage the channel because a "launch-it-and-leave-it" approach will lead to a dead end. This second stage involves overseeing day-to-day content and engagement.

Community Management

Social channels have been likened to the channels that occupy cable TV networks. Each is uniquely designed by its originators to reach a target audience. Social media audiences are very different from their traditional TV counterparts. however, in particular because they have the capacity to create autonomous, and sometimes spontaneous, communities that can alter a channel.

Founding a community takes more than simply putting up a Facebook page or launching a YouTube channel. Initially, it requires recognizing key components:

- Location, which is the channel where the community lives
- Administration, which incorporates the community guidelines set up to moderate behavior on the channel
- Cultural and historical heritage, which becomes evident through the actions and opinions of community members

When people "like" a brand on Facebook, follow it on Twitter, or tag its photos on Instagram, they are not necessarily expressing a particular affinity for either the brand or the channel, but rather for the community and the ideas and beliefs that bind its members. In fact, it is unlikely that a community built around a brand's products or services, or even the brand itself, will attract many devotees.

Those communities that do appeal to significant numbers of users start by defining their ideal members and then fill relevant channels with content that reflects their interests, whether it is music, movies, politics, or sports. In the early stages, it may be necessary to seed the channels with paid media such as Facebook ads and owned media in the form of posts, pins, or tweets. These techniques are continuously used to encourage conversation and social engagement and, if done well, can ultimately grow the network.

Inevitably, a social community is a place where people share their own brand-related stories or seek out those of others. Creating an active and engaged community means having members who are "always on" for a brand and become its day-to-day social bread and butter.

Conversation

What is the role of the channel or community manager today?

Pete Blackshaw, global head of digital and social media, Nestlé: "It's complicated. It is crisis management. It is call center rep. It is content producer, publisher, and now, with all these Facebook innovations, it is media planner. And it is one of those environments where you just can't hand it off to another person. You have to do all of this in a continuous group."

Mandy Gresh, director of brand channel management, Big Fuel: "Part of a channel manager's job is to keep the conversation going between tent poles. The content team develops a big idea, including how it describes itself, the tone of voice, and how a brand should communicate with its audience. Then channel management writes content against that. So while they develop the big idea, channel managers weave the big idea into the content calendar through posts."

Sharon Feder, chief operating officer, Mashable: "What is becoming increasingly important is having people who have creative backgrounds, who could build really dynamic programs that fit the needs of our communities. What this requires are

(continued)

(Continued)

people who are very comfortable with change, who can create a program but also really be able to rework programs, rework the way they handle community tasks when they see that things are not working the way that they should."

Stephanie Agresta, global director of social media and digital, MSLGROUP: "What we're also seeing is how those roles are evolving. The more creative component of managing a community is becoming more important, and that's because of the visual nature of what is becoming engagement. What we are finding now is people are engaging with visual content! Whether it be pictures, infographics, or video. So when you think about a community manager in that context, they become almost like executive producers."

Breaking Through the Clutter

Much as in the "real world," the noise created by myriad social conversations can be virtually deafening. Too many brands still think of social marketing as just another way to pump their messages out to as many people as possible, and the clutter is likely to increase. For example, Gartner estimates that by 2014 as much as 15 percent of social media ratings and reviews will be paid for by companies "scrambling for new ways to build bigger follower bases."[5]

Compounding the problem are brands that believe that more is better when, in fact, less may actually be more. A study by analytics and social marketing firm PageLever found that Facebook pages with more fans garnered fewer unique page views per person.[6] Among pages with between 1,000 and 10,000 fans, daily unique newsfeed impressions were about 1 in 10. Pages with 1 million fans saw their daily unique news feed impressions drop to barely one fourth that, however.

The same is true with respect to the amount of content brands provide. One study shows that just one or two branded Facebook posts a day receive 32 percent more likes and 73 percent more comment rates than posts made three or more times a day.[7]

The most productive social communities start with the premise that success is based on the quality of the content shared, not the quantity. It is a learning process, however, and one that requires brands to think not only like publishers or even networks but, ultimately, like their audiences. Once brands understand the needs and interests of their communities and can tap into those sentiments, they can craft content that is not necessarily what brands dictate, but what the community reacts to.

Keep in Mind . . .

1. A brand's channel architecture is determined by its users' characteristics, their emotional experiences, the media platforms they use, and the channel's recognized function.
2. Within the network model, management responsibilities are divided between channel and community managers.
3. Channel management strategies can be divided into two stages: a broad, campaign-style plan of action and daily content development and engagement.
4. Channel users have the capacity to create autonomous communities that can change the nature of those channels.
5. With respect to the content a channel creates and how often it is shared with a brand's fans, less may be more.

Notes

1. "Campaigns to Capabilities: Social Media and Marketing 2011," Booz and Company/Buddy Media, October 2011, www.booz.com/media/uploads/BoozCo-Campaigns-Capabilities-Social-Media-Marketing.pdf.
2. "Report: Social Demographics in 2012," *Royal Pingdom*, August 21, 2012, http://royal.pingdom.com/2012/08/21/report-social-network-demographics-in-2012/.
3. "The Mindset Divide," LinkedIn, September 12, 2012, http://marketing.linkedin.com/sites/default/files/attachment/MindsetDivide_Infographic.pdf.
4. "The New Multi-screen World: Understanding Cross-platform Consumer Behavior," Google, August 2012, http://services.google.com/fh/files/misc/multiscreenworld_final.pdf.
5. "Gartner Says by 2014, 10–15 Percent of Social Media Reviews to Be Fake, Paid for By Companies," Gartner, Inc., September 17, 2012, www.gartner.com/it/page.jsp?id=2161315.

6. Josh Constine, "Popular Facebook Pages Have Fewer Unique Page Views per Fan, Most Engagement Is in the News Feed," *Inside Facebook*, June 22, 2011, www.insidefacebook.com/2011/06/22/unique-page-views/.

7. "Buddy Media Releases New Research Paper, 'A Statistical Review for the Retail Industry: Strategies for Effective Facebook Wall Posts,'" *Buddy Media*, September 13, 2011, www.buddymedia.com/newsroom/2011/09/buddy-media-releases-new-research-paper-a-statistical-review-for-the-retail-industry-strategies-for-effective-facebook-wall-posts/.

CHAPTER 9

Operations

A growing number of companies now recognize that social media has, or will soon become, a vital part of their business operations. Fewer, though, yet realize just how important efficient operations are to social media.

Operations, as a practice, serves as a combined skeletal and nervous system of a brand network, ensuring that channel architecture is set up properly and that all the dynamic aspects of the brand strategy work together to produce optimum results. At the heart of operations are the separate but interconnected processes that govern both the day-to-day activities that keep a network running as well as the strategies and campaigns that must be consistently achieved over the span of weeks, months, and even years. The most essential of these operations will be detailed throughout much of the rest of this book. Two other central components—technology and talent—are also key to the success of every social brand network.

Technology

"Social media runs on technology," says Michoel Ogince, Big Fuel's director of platform and product strategy. "It is the DNA of social media marketing." Unlike the biological genetic molecule that slowly evolves over millennia, however, social technologies can change seemingly overnight, forcing organizations to perpetually think both short and long term about investing in appropriate applications.

Ogince oversees Social Labs, Big Fuel's innovation division, which was first established in response to the ongoing proliferation of products and vendors that overpopulate conversational marketing. Brands of all shapes and sizes need to work with varying casts of technology partners to develop and deploy timely solutions to equally varied problems. For agencies like Big Fuel that serve a broad array of clients, the task can be even more daunting. That is why Ogince and his team spend a significant part of each day researching, reviewing, and experimenting with all sorts of new hardware and software.

Few brands have the resources or personnel to keep their heads constantly above the flood of current and emerging systems as do firms like Big Fuel, nor does any one company typically require the number of different solutions that Big Fuel's diverse clients do. All brands none-theless share a universal need to find the right tool for the right job. "The more we know about what a particular technology can and can't do," says Ogince, "the more effectively we can marry that technology to a campaign or particular brand objective."

The process starts by understanding what a brand is trying to accomplish before considering any specific technology. It may be listening and learning, conversing, creating content, or measuring the effect of all the above. Obviously, such objectives differ from brand to brand. Moreover, a single brand can also change goals from campaign to campaign or even from circumstance to circumstance.

When the purpose is determined, the brand can then look outward to identify and evaluate the most suitable products and vendors. At this point, platforms can be categorized into different functionalities, such as back-end capabilities, front-end user experiences, API protocols, and social features. It is also important—especially if a brand plans to partner with a vendor—to go beyond the sales team to the persons who created and maintain the application so as to guarantee not just their existing knowledge and skills, but also their capacity to make any necessary adjustments or changes. Once technologies and processes are in place, attention turns to those who will implement both.

Talent

Social media is an octopus. This notion is worth repeating because just about every facet of marketing and communications is touched by social media, and every one of those touch points requires someone who knows how to manage it.

"One of the ongoing challenges every brand faces is training and developing their people," notes Big Fuel's chief talent officer Anthony Onesto. "It is such a dynamic market that everyone in every organization constantly has to relearn how to adapt." Although there is a need for multiple types of knowledge and skills, several transcend almost all social brands:

- Being creative across all disciplines, even disciplines not usually associated with creativity, such as project management
- Having a passion for social, which doesn't necessarily mean being significantly experienced in it, but certainly being active at it
- Doing the best to stay ahead of the curve

Conversation

If you were running a brand and looking to put together a team that can drive social media behavior and create branded content, what kind of team would you put together?

Ted Rubin, chief social marketing officer, Collective Bias: "It is different for every company. Major corporations will spend the money it takes to have a total top-down organization, while smaller businesses will have to rely on different people in different departments, such as the social guy for production, the social guy for management, and the social guy for communications and marketing."

Pete Blackshaw, global head of digital and social media, Nestlé: "There are a couple different paths you can go down. You can look for that digital social vertical specialist: someone who has done digital CRM [customer relationship management] or social media execution, and who knows social content management systems. We all need people like that. But increasingly, what I really want are great brand builders who understand digital, because I think if you hire a great brand builder, they are going to go ga-ga over digital listening tools, because they are consumer nuts and they like whatever lets them

(continued)

(*Continued*)

get closer to the consumer. And I think it is less complicated than it was before in part because everyone is surrounded by social and doing it all the time. You're not showing them social. You're just showing them a better way of understanding the consumer."

Rubin: "One of the first types of people I would look for are listeners. And I want two types of listeners. I want data listeners who know how to use the tools and read what comes out of the tools, and garner valuable information from that. Then I want talented listeners who can integrate themselves into a group and really pay attention. And I want two types of those people: the ones who can do it internally in the organization and those who can do it with customers."

Stephanie Agresta, global director of social media and digital, MSLGROUP: "I am starting to feel more and more as I hire, that I want to hire people who come from multiple disciplines. I have found that the greatest success when we build teams of people with different talent, expertise, and experience in social and digital. This diversity of talent is critical to solving problems in social."

Herb Scannell, president, BBC Worldwide America at BBC Worldwide: "The truth about an executive's job is you're really, you're a champion; if you were anything more than that, you'd be doing it yourself. When you're a leader, you lead by initiative and you lead by championing. And if you're putting together a team, you should champion people that can do things that you might not be able to do."

The complex social media system is also comprised of individuals who can help a brand through various processes and who work together to guide a brand across the entire network. They make up the network team.

The Network Team

At Big Fuel we have spent considerable time and energy thinking about the right team construct to best service the needs of our clients. Knowing that social media "touches" every part of an organization requires our teams to be organized slightly differently from a traditional agency.

Network Director

In the network model, the network director's is "the one throat to choke." It is the network director's job to oversee the administrative structure of the entire network and to provide the direction and vision for each brand campaign. All roads lead here, and the network director is in charge of seeing to it that everything that needs doing gets done.

A strong network director has to be a know-it-all. That is, she has to know a brand's business inside and out. Just as important, she has to fully understand her own responsibilities, including what, when, and how to delegate to the appropriate members of the team. In addition, she sets both the tone and the example for how best to work with those outside of her team, such as customer service, marketing communications, public relations, and a host of different agencies.

Although the network director is the team's big-picture person who gets to such answer questions as "What role does social play?" and "What can social accomplish?" she also supervises the day-to-day performance of the network and tracks its impact on a brand's revenue growth. These responsibilities put her at the center of the network model.

Network Manager

One or more network managers or coordinators support the network director. They make up the operational core of the team and look after the daily details of running the network as well as all of its associated programs and campaigns. They also provide linkage from one day to the next by running regular integrated team meetings that review prior accomplishments and glitches.

Program Director

Serving essentially as a partner to the network director, the program director is primarily responsible for ensuring that the right people are assigned to the work at hand. He is also tasked with managing the financials for all projects and campaigns, including relationships with vendors. In addition, should any issues arise regarding delivery of services, he is the escalation point person for dealing with them.

Program Manager

As the operational leader for on-time campaign delivery, the program manager ensures that a brand's needs are correctly articulated to the channel management team members so that deliverables and commitments are clearly understood. The program manager's responsibilities include maintaining accurate weekly client status and measurement reports.

Director of Audience Insights

The director of audience insights leads audience, channel, and metrics planning to establish a concise vision of audience habits and traits—such as where and when they are likely to engage with brand content. This director subsequently works to set thresholds for key performance indicators (KPIs).

Strategist

Along with developing strategic plans, defining KPIs and social brand objectives is the strategist's job. Central to the strategist's role is ensuring that all creative work aligns with brand goals.

Analyst

Working with the lead strategist, the analyst represents the research arm of the audience insights team. By conducting primary and secondary research, the analyst owns both the quantitative and qualitative data that inform overall brand strategy.

Director of Channel Management

The director of channel management is the person responsible for overall community management and engagement across the entire network. Working closely with the content team to brainstorm channel posting strategies, the director develops curated content calendars that guide the daily activities and objectives for the channel and community managers.

Channel Manager

The channel manager's job is to define the role and content for each channel a brand owns. This manager works closely with the client on content calendar approval as well as on identifying, defining, and activating escalation plans when emergencies arise. This person is the key point of contact for customer care and customer service and oversees community managers who live day-to-day in the channels.

Community Manager

Consistently monitoring agreed-upon channels regularly engaging and responding to consumers is the job of a community manager. This person writes content, works with the designer for lightweight image creation, and executes all posts. The community manager is always monitoring for potential issues, which are then raised to the network team and clients' attention.

Content Director

The content director is the creative lead across the entire brand network. The equivalent of a creative director in typical agency constructs, the content director is responsible for creating social programs to meet client business and marketing directives and acts as creative point of contact to clients and other agencies.

Keep in Mind . . .

1. Operations is the spine of a brand network that ensures all aspects of its strategy effectively work together.
2. Processes govern a network's daily activities, along with its long-term strategies and campaigns.
3. To choose the most appropriate applications from among an ever-expanding range of technologies, brands must first define their specific objectives and then evaluate products and vendors based on their abilities to consistently meet challenges, no matter how circumstances change.
4. Although social knowledge and skills may vary from brand to brand, the common dominators are creativity, a passion for social, and the capacity to stay ahead of the curve.

SECTION III

Audience First

CHAPTER 10

Building Bridges

O f all the aspects of a complex social media system, probably none is more perplexing than an increasingly global audience that divides and subdivides itself along geographic, economic, social, cultural, political, gender, age, ethnic, and even religious distinctions. These disparities affect not only what kinds of content audiences access, but also how they access it and how they interpret it. Nothing distinguishes social media from traditional forms of marketing more than the changing relationships between brands and these diverse audiences.

Social Is Global

At the end of 2012, more than 1.5 billion people on the planet were using social media, and 6 in 10 of them regularly connected with social networks, forums, or blogs.[1] The percentage of social media users in more than a dozen countries is greater than that of the United States (Figure 10.1), and in many parts of the world they are more willing to engage with brands. In China, for example, more than half of all Internet users say that they would buy a product or service because someone they knew "liked" or followed it online.[2] That response dwarfs the 15 percent of Americans who would do the same.

There is also a good deal of diversity within the United States itself. Women use social media more than men, younger users usually spend more time online than their elders, and Hispanic adults are 25 percent more likely to follow a brand than the general online population.

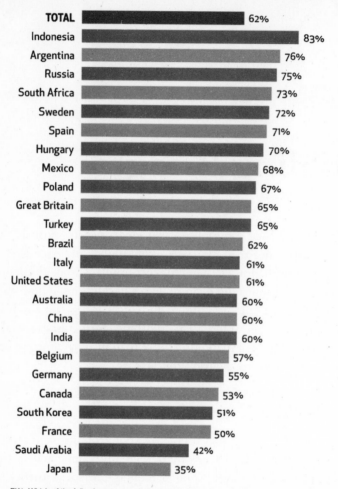

EK1. Which of the following purposes have you used the Internet for in the past three months?
Base: All Respondents *n* = 19,216

An Ipsos Global @dvisory—March 2012—G@30 | TECH TRACKER

Figure 10.1   Nations Visiting Social Networking Sites

Nonetheless, these many differences still do not close the gap that often separates consumers from the brands that wish to reach them.

Passion Points

The great divide between brands and consumers should come as no surprise because most brands still base their communication with consumers almost solely on the messages they plan to deliver and the

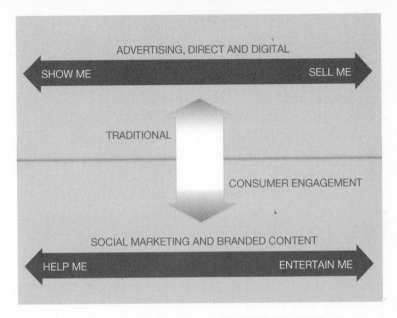

Figure 10.2 Consumer Engagement and Traditional Marketing

outcomes they hope to achieve. In other words, they emphasize "show and sell." Consequently, they make themselves and what they want the focus of their attention. This strategy embodies what we call traditional or commerce-based marketing (Figure 10.2).

Consumers, however, have an entirely different agenda. They often know little, and probably care less, if any particular piece of content is paid for through an agency, earned with the help of a public relations firm, or owned by whomever created it. Rather, they are perpetually on the lookout for anything that will help them find, learn, do something of value, or just keep them entertained. Above all, they are drawn to content that stirs their intellect or emotions. Those passion points are at the heart of social or content-based marketing.

What kinds of products are consumers really passionate about? Probably toothpaste and yogurt are not high on the list. Some brands may be preferable to others, but they rarely generate a great deal of excitement. On the other hand, many people are impassioned by automobiles. Even so, it is not necessarily a specific car model or its features that attracts consumers. What galvanizes consumers is the speed, mobility, and power that different models and features exude, whether they experience them on their own behind the wheel or watch cathartically as race cars maneuver a NASCAR track or the Indy 500. The content that can tap into such experiences is what truly connects with audiences.

Perhaps no other brand has been more successful at capturing consumers' passions than Apple. Its iPods, iPhones, and iPads have sparked the imagination of people all over the world for years. Again, though, it is not so much the products themselves that seduce most fans, nor is it that the products are mobile. After all, the Sony Walkman and the first laptop computer provided such portability long ago. Rather, because Apple products are gateways to unique and valued content—music, movies, games, and more—they promote engagement and engender loyalty.

A Lot to Learn

If at its core social media marketing is about genuinely connecting with consumers through compelling content, the problem for most brands is twofold. First, as noted above, they are frequently unaware of what actually matters to consumers. They want to sell their products and do not care much about the story in the newspaper, the music playing on the radio, or the program airing on TV that accompanies their ads even though the story, music, or program can provide them with a direct link to a trove of invaluable insights.

Second, even when brands are mindful of their customers, they are not all that sure about how to act on it. According to research by IBM, the vast majority (80 percent) of companies surveyed are eager to interact with their customers wherever they congregate online, and are aggressively launching social media initiatives.[3] Yet fewer than one-third are confident they have implemented the kinds of strategies that will help guarantee success. This lack of confidence is because most brands are, at best, tourists in the land of content. It is not a business they know, at least not well. What they understand is how to place media and then pay for it. What they do not understand is how to tell meaningful stories to targeted audiences (Figure 10.3).

Too many companies still think in terms of what social scientists refer to as representative agents: factitious persons or groups who typify the behavior of broad swaths of the population. For marketers, they may be women age 18 to 49, men age 25 to 54, or a whole host of other demographic classifications. In the past, broadcasting mass commercial messages may have seemed like an effective way to reach them, but that method is much less effective in today's social media landscape.

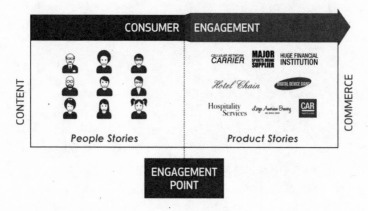

Figure 10.3 Connecting Content to Commerce

The problem is that most consumers do not see themselves that way. They tend to think of themselves as unique individuals, and they increasingly enjoy connecting with other distinct individuals. So, brands must learn to plug in to such conversations with content that rouses consumers' passions and is consistent with their activities and expectations on social networks.

How do they do that? They do not use conventional, or even digital, advertising techniques; those are still essentially about the brand. Instead, they have to focus on their audience and build bridges that connect to what consumers truly care about.

Conversation

How can brands learn to be successful content creators?

Pete Blackshaw, global head of digital and social media, Nestlé: "Historically, brands just have too much advertising in the model, so what they have to try to figure out is a nonbranded entry point that may be a lot easier for catching consumers. And intuitively, that makes sense. If you look at Google Search behavior, only 1 percent of all the searches are branded. Most consumers enter through more of a category/life

(continued)

(Continued)

stage entry point, and I think that creates real complexity and challenge but also huge opportunities for the brands that get that right."

Sharon Feder, chief operating officer, Mashable: "When I look at content, I think that it is very much in line with social in that you need to understand what your community is looking for, what is valuable to them, and what they want to consume. And I think one of the most interesting things about both social and content is that all of this is measurable. So we can look to data. We can look to sentiment and understand what's working and what's not for our particular communities. And I think that when it comes to content, just as it's become standard for brands to be on social, it's become standard for brands to be content creators."

Blackshaw: "Message quality still really matters in the digital world. And in fact, it may matter even more because the upside and the downside are intensified around messaging. If your message totally sucks, you are going get punished disproportionately. So everything that kind of goes into the right message is more important than ever. At Nestlé, we look at messaging as three buckets. First, we want to minimize avoidance and rejection from consumers. Second, we also want to maximize impact, sociability, and sharing. And finally, we want to figure out how to do that consistently in its scale."

Keep in Mind . . .

1. In a global economy, brands have to learn how to communicate with increasingly diverse audiences.
2. Brands must shift their perspective from focusing on their own products and services (commerce-based marketing) to addressing the needs and interests of consumers (content-based marketing).
3. To that end, brands must also learn how to touch audiences' passion points through interesting and meaningful stories.

Notes

1. "Interconnected World: Communication and Networking," Ipsos, March 27, 2012, www.ipsos-na.com/news-polls/pressrelease.aspx?id=5564.

2. "Consumers in Asia-Pacific More Responsive to Social Endorsements," *eMarketer*, July 16, 2012, www.emarketer.com/Article.aspx?R=1009190&ecid=a6506033675 d47f881651943c21c5ed4.

3. IBM Institute for Business Value, "From Social Media to Social CRM: Reinventing the Customer Relationship," IBM, June 2011, http://public.dhe.ibm.com/common/ssi/ecm/en/gbe03416usen/GBE03416USEN.PDF.

CHAPTER 11

Welcome to the Party

In the world of social media, communication is akin to conversation. Conversations are mutual interactions. *A* says something to *B*, *B* responds, and so begins a dialogue. If they know each other well or if the parameters of their relationship are clear, their discourse will go much as expected. If not, it is apt to be unpredictable, possibly uncontrollable, and almost always self-adjusting.

Now multiply that practically infinitely. To be sure, no single person or organization can adequately converse with hundreds of friends or millions of followers, but given that 8 in 10 people on the Internet now regularly connect through social media,[1] the ability to take part in these innumerable exchanges largely defines today's social communication.

Meeting Expectations

Consumers aren't necessarily eager to chat with every brand they encounter in the social sphere. To the contrary, more than half have never even considered engaging a company via social media.[2] Those who do, however, prefer that much of their communication be in the form of conversations. In fact, more than 80 percent believe that companies should respond to customers if they ask a question or file a complaint on a social site.[3]

Just as important, more than half expect a response within 24 hours. Sadly, only 29 percent ever get one.[4] Even more lamentable is that 70 percent of questions posted by brands' Facebook fans are ignored

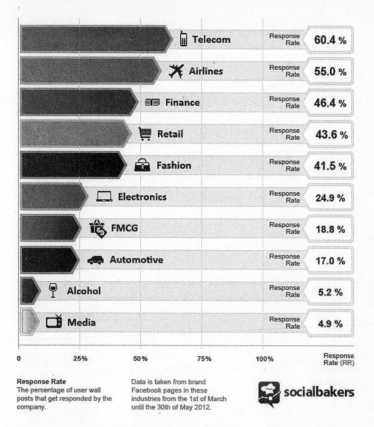

Figure 11.1   The Most Socially Devoted Industries on Facebook

entirely, with one in four global companies going as far as to make their walls private to avoid queries.[5] The response rate varies considerably among industries, from telecommunications firms that respond to more than 60 percent of posts to media companies that all but ignore their fans (Figure 11.1).

Refusing to engage with consumers across social media is not just poor etiquette, but bad business. Such was the finding of a 2011 customer experience impact (CEI) study conducted by Harris Interactive.[6] The research found that just 1 percent of consumers surveyed believe that their expectations for good customer service are always met. As for the remaining 99 percent, half give a brand no more than a week to respond to their questions; when no answer is forthcoming, most choose to go elsewhere—often to a competitor. Before doing so, however, one in four lets others know about his/her experience by posting a negative comment on a social media site.

The CEI study also concluded that when companies are willing to engage with their customers, the payoff can be significant. Eighty-six percent of consumers said that they would actually spend more with a brand if they could be guaranteed better customer service. Nonetheless, not even a fifth of businesses that were queried for a separate study by German software firm SAP used social media to address a fourth or more of their customer service issues.[7]

Insight

As a former chief marketing executive at Intelliseek, BuzzMetrics, and Nielsen Online, Pete Blackshaw has spent more than a decade examining brand advocacy and influencer management.

[A lot of companies] are really bad at consumer services, because all the incentives have been aligned around fewer consumers through the pipe, and less time for consumers. And that is very much at odds with social media. And I think for any of us to be credible in the conversation, we're going to have to look across the entire value chain. And that is complicated, because brands have to ask themselves really hard operational questions.

Brands shouldn't be focusing on media amplification if they can't make it easier for consumers to give a brand a direct high-five. I've worked with hundreds of brands and analyzed countless conversations, and what I have generally found is that there is a huge correlation between screwing up with core service operations and considerable pain on Facebook or Twitter. It's a very direct correlation. So I don't think brands really have a right to go hang out welcome mats on Facebook until they get those core fundamentals right.

Insight

Ted Rubin is a leading social marketing strategist as well as creator and evangelist of the concept of return on relationship, which is also the title of his book.

Whenever I was a CMO at a company, there were two people I made best friends with. One was the chief technology officer, or one of the technology people who could fix a problem for me. The other was the customer service person. If I am out there shouting on behalf of the brand and building relationships, in one fell swoop customer service can ruin all that because their job is about dollars and cents, about measuring how many calls and how long it takes to get a call answered, and how cheaply can we do it. Which means their message is completely different. So I made sure to do two things: Make friends with them and spend time with them the same way we do with customers to influence them to the point [where] they understood the relationship between marketing and customer service.

Welcome to the Party

For brands doing business across social channels, one of the keys to success is to understand how best to interact with consumers. What part of the consumer experience is it appropriate for the brand to talk about? Where does the brand have the credibility to come in and take part in a conversation?

To that end, it helps to think of social media as a party where multiple conversations take place concurrently. Some happen in isolation, and others cross-pollinate as talkers traverse from one group to another. It may be working moms in one corner of the room discussing education or parenting skills, sports fans in another sizing up Super Bowl contenders, or teens somewhere else speculating on the fate of the *Twilight* saga. Each group is unique, and anyone hoping to join their conversations must be prepared to do so on the group's terms.

Listen First, Sell Later

The first and most important prerequisite is to listen. Context is everything. The same topic can have significantly different meanings when discussed by diverse people in varying circumstances. Knowing what is truly important in a conversation is crucial before jumping in. Once in, the trick is to stay relevant.

Marketers face the same challenges online. There is no shortage of details from which to cull insights about consumers today. With the growing dominance of social media and the share of data generated, brands can extract valuable insights from the trillions upon trillions of bits of information generated by both people and machines. By examining massive amounts of data simultaneously across hundreds or thousands of parallel servers, companies can discover once-shrouded paradigms among consumer behaviors and then respond in real time.

A brand's responses are also defined by its intentions, however. If its initial objective is to sell its wares, it will likely be greeted online like a huckster at a party would, with complete dismissal. According to NM Incite, a principal reason people give up friends on Facebook is because the friends in question try to sell them something.[8] Too often, that is exactly what companies attempt to do.

Selling is embedded in all marketers' DNA, and they have been taught, practically from day one, to always lead with their "product story," distilling their message down to a unique selling proposition and driving it home with features and benefits. In the past, this strategy has worked well, especially if they have only 30 seconds to pitch a product through an ad that is blasted out into the world on TV, radio, or elsewhere.

Whether joining a conversation or starting one from scratch, a new entrant will find few responses if the talk is solely about his own self interests. To engage consumers, brands cannot initiate a meaningful dialogue through "product stories"; rather, they need "people stories" that arouse passions and can be readily adapted, no matter who is on the other end of the exchange. According to a poll of 24 nations carried out by global research services firm Ipsos, more than half of social network users worldwide prefer that ads served via their social pages are tailored to their personal interests.[9]

Conversation

What does it take for brands to have meaningful conversations with consumers via social media?

Herb Scannell, president, BBC Worldwide America at BBC Worldwide: "You have to respect your audience. Make sure that you are consistent across the conversations and dialogues you have with your audience, and that you take that into consideration when you're doing whatever it is you are doing online. Everything is about respecting an audience, because no matter what the medium, respect goes a long way."

Rikard Steiber, global marketing director of mobile and social advertising, Google: "Sometimes you don't have all the answers like you probably have as a publisher, but you are starting a discussion and the forum might actually come up with an answer that might be a different way to think about publishing going forward."

Ted Rubin, chief social marketing officer, Collective Bias: "Give people something to hold on to. Give them something that makes them want to say they enjoy their experience. And when they don't, that's okay too. I think brands should be open to negative comments. You take the kudos when you do good and the crap when you are not delivering what they want!"

The Opening Line

Catering to users' personal interests means starting with the right opening line: an engagement point through which to enter a conversation that recognizes consumers' inclinations and plays to them. Miss that, and the conversation is over before it begins. That is something Société BIC learned the hard way.

When the company, best known for its writing implements, launched its BIC Cristal for Her ballpoint pens, it promoted the product on Amazon as "an elegant design—just for her," with its "diamond-

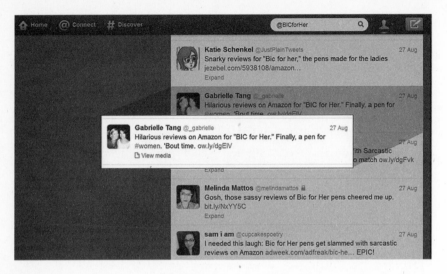

Figure 11.2   Twitter Conversation

engraved barrel for an elegant and unique feminine style." In no time, scores of consumers assailed the page with a barrage of sarcastic comments. One snarky five-star review read:

> *Someone has answered my gentle prayers and FINALLY designed a pen that I can use all month long! I use it when I'm swimming, riding a horse, walking on the beach, and doing yoga. It's comfortable, leak-proof, nonslip, and it makes me feel so feminine and pretty! Since I've begun using these pens, men have found me more attractive and approachable. It has given me soft skin and manageable hair and it has really given me the self-esteem I needed to start a book club and flirt with the bag boy at my local market.*

To make matters worse, the company failed to contain the problem and allowed its critics to secure @BICforHer on Twitter. There, it was the target of additional lampooning (Figure 11.2).

The Right Fit

Of course, even the best opening line can only go so far in enabling a conversation. At some point, it is also essential to establish a level of credibility, a reason others should not only listen to what is being said, but believe it. It is worth repeating that context is everything. If there is a disconnect between the message and how the messenger is perceived, the conversation is still doomed to fail, great opening lines notwithstanding.

Among all the advertisers during the 2012 Summer Olympics, none generated more talk than McDonald's, which was the subject of nearly one in every four sponsor-related comments.[10] Unfortunately for the brand, many of those comments questioned the role of the fast-food chain as an appropriate sponsor for an athletic event. Despite its level of social media outreach (McDonald's maintains a team of tweeters to regularly chat with consumers), it took a drubbing on Twitter, where it scored between minus 70,000 and minus 100,000 on MediaCom's Daily Olympic Twitter Tracker.[11]

Influencers and Advocates

At any large gathering—online or off—it is useful to have someone on hand who can draw people's attention. In real-world social settings, this person is generally the life of the party. On social networks, this person is an "influencer." The most powerful influencers have thousands of Twitter followers and generate millions of Facebook likes. Given their stature, they may be handsomely compensated by brands in return for helping make products go viral. Beyond their ability to attract eyeballs, however, many influencers' real clout may not be determined only by their Klout scores.

Among those who challenge the conventional wisdom about influencers is Duncan Watts, a principal research scientist for Microsoft. As early as 2001, he began questioning the notion that one person or a small group of people can drive collective purchasing behaviors online. Additional findings by social platforms BuzzFeed and StumbleUpon assert that when influential people do reach a wide audience, their impact is short lived.[12] Moreover, results have shown that content is more likely to spread when large numbers of ordinary people share it with small groups of other ordinary people instead of when it comes from someone "special."

Watts has taken it a step further. He maintains that regardless of who the sender is, the flood of ideas will only flow if the receivers are a critical mass of easily influenced people who will then pass the information to other easy-to-influence people. Subsequent research of Facebook users by New York University economists Sinan Aral and Dylan Walker concluded that younger users are more easily influenced than older users, men are more influential than women, and married couples are the least susceptible to other opinions when adopting products.[13]

The truth about influencers' abilities to lead, and the willingness of others to follow, is still open to debate, but emerging is a gradual shift in focus from influencers to "advocates." The latter are people who use and spread the word about products and services without being asked. They are "true believers," and although they may not garner as many adherents as influencers, they tend to engender greater trust. The same can be said for brands. Among consumers who interact with companies online, the majority favors those who are honest in their communications.[14]

These findings should come as no surprise. In person or online, the most successful conversations are those firmly grounded in sincerity, understanding, and relevance.

Keep in Mind . . .

1. Most consumers do not have good customer experiences with brands, even though research shows that they would be willing to pay more for better service.
2. Brands that use social media have numerous opportunities to listen to consumers carefully and gain valuable insights about their needs and behaviors.
3. To engage consumers, brands need to create "people stories" that arouse their audiences' interests rather than "product stories" that are essentially sales messages.
4. If there is a disparity between what a brand is trying to communicate and how consumers perceive it, the message will not get through.
5. When used effectively, influencers and advocates can help brands open doors to consumers.

Notes

1. Michael Chui, James Manyika, Jacques Bughin, Richard Dobbs, Charles Roxburgh, Hugo Sarrazin, Geoffrey Sands, and Magdalena Westergren, "The Social Economy: Unlocking Value and Productivity through Social Technologies," McKinsey Global Institute, McKinsey and Company, July 2012, www.mckinsey.com/insights/mgi/research/technology_and_innovation/the_social_economy.

2. IBM Institute for Business Value, "From Social Media to Social CRM: What Customers Want," IBM, February 2011, http://public.dhe.ibm.com/common/ssi/ecm/en/gbe03391usen/GBE03391USEN.PDF.

3. Harry Rollason, "Social Media Has Changed the Face of Customer Service as We Know It, for Good," Useful Social Media, August 8, 2012, http://usefulsocialmedia.com/blog/customer-service/social-media-has-changed-the-face-of-customer-service-as-we-know-it-for-good/.

4. Ibid.

5. Jan Rezab, "70% of Fans Are Being Ignored by Companies—Now What?" Socialbakers, June 20, 2012, www.socialbakers.com/blog/655-70-of-fans-are-being-ignored-by-companies-now-what.

6. "2011 Customer Experience Impact Report: Getting to the Heart of the Consumer and Brand Relationship," Oracle Corporation, 2012, www.oracle.com/us/products/applications/cust-exp-impact-report-epss-1560493.pdf.

7. "The Social Customer Engagement Index 2012: Results, Analysis and Perspectives," October 16, 2012, http://podcasts.socialmediatoday.com/media/sap_wp_assets/TheSocialCustomerEngagementIndex_2012.pdf.

8. Nielsen Company, "Friends and Frenemies: Why We Add and Remove Facebook Friends," *Nielsen Wire*, December 19, 2011, http://blog.nielsen.com/nielsenwire/online_mobile/friends-frenemies-why-we-add-and-remove-facebook-friends/.

9. "Who's in Favor of Targeted Social Media Ads?" MarketingProfs, October 26, 2012, www.marketingprofs.com/charts/2012/9198/whos-in-favor-of-targeted-social-media-ads.

10. Steve McClellan, "Olympics Earn Positive Social Media, McDonald's Slammed as Sponsor," *Online Media Daily*, August 31, 2012, www.mediapost.com/publications/article/181984/olympics-earn-positive-social-media-mcdonalds-sl.html.

11. Mark Sweeney, "Olympic Brand McDonald's Suffers Twitter Humiliation," *The Guardian*, July 12, 2012, www.guardian.co.uk/media/2012/jul/27/olympic-brand-mcdonalds-twitter.

12. Jack Krawczyk and Jon Steinberg, "How Content Is Really Shared: Close Friends, Not 'Influencers,' " *Ad Age Digital*, March 7, 2012.

13. Sinan Aral and Dylan Walker, "Identifying Influential and Susceptible Members of Social Networks," *Science* 337 (2012): 337–341, doi: 10.1126/science.1215842.

14. IBM Institute for Business Value, "From Social Media to Social CRM."

CHAPTER 12

Mutual Priorities

There is probably nothing brands want more from social media than to have consumers talk about them. Unfortunately, most consumers do not share this view. The majority of global executives surveyed by IBM believe that social will increase customer advocacy.[1] Yet fewer than one in four consumers agree.

In traditional marketing, brands provide information that reflects their priorities. They create content, find an audience, place a media buy, and broadcast messages that attempt to sell their products or services. For their part, consumers increasingly want to get information that reflects their priorities. It is not that they refuse to be sold to, but at the very least, they want brands to be transparent about it.[2]

In Sync

The challenge for brands, then, is to sync priorities by learning how to take part in conversations that spark audiences' interests. Occasionally, they get lucky and ignite something, but luck is not a sustainable strategy. Brands that consistently succeed do so because they know how to square their prerogatives with consumers' behaviors and expectations. Despite several previous chapters explaining why many of the old rules of marketing no longer apply to social, there are still a few that do. One of them is: Use the right channel for the right message.

Most social followership comes from consumers who have an existing relationship with a brand.[3] They are either current users or former users who have had positive experiences and expect to use that brand again. The public relations firm Edelman conducted research among Millennials in eight countries—including the United States, China, India, and Brazil—and found that 70 percent believe that once they deal with a company or product they like, they will keep coming back.[4] In addition, more than half are willing to share additional personal information with a trusted brand in return for more relevant content.

Consequently, brands can in large part set their priorities based on what they learn from consumers. According to McKinsey, companies that leverage consumer insights for product development and marketing can create added value by engaging with audiences on social media and monitoring their conversations. By integrating social strategies with those of other channels—consumer packaged goods brands, for example—a company can create value equivalent to between 15 and 30 percent of its current marketing and development spending.[5]

Stick to the Point

Identifying and understanding what is truly important to consumers does not keep some brands from trying to insert extraneous information into conversations. Included here are unrelated advertising, events, product announcements, or press releases, some of which are not especially pertinent to marketing objectives but, rather, are available inventory that is easy to add to an editorial calendar. At this point, the grid comes into play again.

As a general rule, if something is not on the grid, it probably does not align with anything else being done. Occasional outliers or tangential topics may appear, especially as a result of rapidly changing circumstances, but just as in real conversations, non sequiturs do not enhance engagement. Unless a person announces that she is straying far off topic, there is a pregnant pause before conversation either picks up again or dies.

The same often happens in social media. A brand may join in ongoing exchanges with target audiences and compile a consistent engagement rate only to lose both by going off topic or pulling new information out of nowhere. At best, the content will be ignored. At worst, it will generate a lot of negative sentiment because no one can figure out why it is there. If entirely new or distinctly different ideas must be included, one way to do so is to prepare well in advance; then, use tent poles to gradually introduce the information and attempt to build original conversations around them.

Setting successful priorities is essentially a matter of perspective. Brands that fail to recognize what is important to consumers may find themselves in competition with the very people they are trying to reach. On the other hand, those willing to see their audiences as their audiences see themselves will develop long-term and commercially valuable relationships. Often, it all comes down to the ability to listen.

Keep in Mind . . .

1. A critical challenge for social marketers is to match their brand's priorities with those of their current and potential customers.
2. To do so, they must continually listen and learn from consumers.
3. By using the grid as a guide to how to connect with consumers, brands can avoid including irrelevant content.

Notes

1. IBM Institute for Business Value, "From Social Media to Social CRM: What the Customer Wants," IBM, February 2011, http://public.dhe.ibm.com/common/ssi/ecm/en/gbe03391usen/GBE03391USEN.PDF.
2. Ibid. Of consumers surveyed by IBM, the majority who said that they are willing to interact with brands will do so only if they believe that the company is communicating with them honestly.
3. Ibid.
4. Edelman, "The 8095 Exchange: Millennials, Their Actions Surrounding Brands, and the Dynamics of Reverberation," *SlideShare*, last modified October 14, 2010, www.slideshare.net/StrategyOne/8095-whitepaper.
5. McKinsey Global Institute, "The Social Economy: Unlocking Value and Productivity through Social Technologies," McKinsey & Company, July 2012, www.mckinsey.com/insights/mgi/research/technology_and_innovation/the_social_economy.

CHAPTER 13

Audience Insights

C onsider the various ways brands have been urged to think about themselves: as publishers, as networks, and, of course, as marketers of their products and services. As terms such as engagement and concepts like consumer control permeate the social sphere, though, thinking like the audience is becoming a paramount condition for success.

There is certainly no shortage of consumer-related information to sort through. To the contrary, website traffic, online searches, banner advertising, social media, and smartphone use leave behind vast trails of personal data. It is estimated, for example, that 34,000 tweets are sent every minute. That comes to about 1 billion tweets per month, which is still far less than the 30 billion pieces of content posted on Facebook.[1]

Under the rubric of big data, growing numbers of companies are collecting all they can in hope that by tracking individuals throughout the purchase funnel—from interested party to eventual customer—they can generalize strategies for reaching a great many others. So far, however, the results have been mixed. Of a global sample of marketers queried by researchers at Econsultancy and web analytics firm Lynchpin, only 1 in 10 found the majority of their data helpful in making decisions.[2]

Mashing Up Strategy and Analytics

In most forms of marketing, strategy and analytics occupy separate spaces. The conventional planning process often starts with considerable and expensive survey-based research—or ongoing tracking studies—designed to explore consumer sentiment about a brand, its products, the landscape in which it operates, and its ability to effectively convey its message or positioning theme. Other techniques might be used to investigate consumers' motivations and behaviors up and down the purchase funnel.[3]

At the same time, the brand's media agency may run similarly expensive research in parallel to identify demographic and psychographic indicators and indexes meant to tell its client just who and how the brand should target its paid advertising and audience planning. The results might yield something like the following:

- Men age 25 to 54 who live in urban areas have a high propensity to adopt new technology before the rest of the country.
- The brand's product range has low awareness compared to more established competitors among this demographic.
- The target indexes at 126 against "willing to try new things when it comes to personal communication systems."

The findings are then passed to the strategy team members, who put them into play. Then the outcomes are measured against earlier expectations.

There is no doubt that this approach can deliver some interesting analysis and be useful in tracking a brand's health, yet this type of sweeping, ground-up investigation and the conclusions drawn from it are unlikely to capture many of the rapid changes that define today's global economy. Nor can one simply leverage such knowledge from one year to the next. To do so requires merging analytics and strategy into a single, ongoing process, as described by Stuart Schwartzapfel, Big Fuel's vice president of audience insights:

> *Audience Insights is a mashup of strategy and analytics. Traditionally, they are separate departments, but we have brought them together because we believe having either of them exist in a vacuum doesn't make any sense. We always want to be strategic. We always want to optimize our work with data and analytics. But when they were previously separate, we learned that wasn't working for anybody.*

Insight

Reggie Bradford served as chief marketing officer of WebMD during the late 1990s.

When I was a brand manager we had focus groups and we would sit behind the clouded glass in a major city and hear people who were paid fifty or a hundred dollars to talk about our ad campaigns, our brand, our positioning, or whatever the case might be. But what you have now is such a more powerful opportunity to create those direct dialogues every single day; and to study and understand consumer behavior, sentiment, and the conversations that are happening around your brand on your social properties. And I think it is those brand managers who leverage the conversations, and learn from them, who are going to be in such demand, because they now have better tools than I had at my disposal in the late nineties.

Take the Time to Listen

For generations, marketers have wielded an array of tools to measure consumer attitudes and behaviors. One way or another, though, they have been hampered by the size of the sample, the persons chosen, the kinds of questions asked, or the manner in which they are asked. Differences in the tools themselves have also skewed results, as was made clear during the 2012 elections. In several polls that used automated telephone dialing, or robo-calling, and that were strictly limited to landline phones, Mitt Romney was often even or ahead in the race for president. Polls in states such as Ohio, Florida, and Virginia, which included calls to cell phones and made use of live interviewers, put Barack Obama in the lead, however.[4]

Equally inhibiting is that many brands focus their inquiries around their own products or services, missing opportunities to learn what is really important to both existing and potential customers. Granted, product messaging serves a more crucial role as consumers get closer to the point of purchase, but what happens when they are not yet in market? What is the best way to keep them engaged before, during, and after the purchase? Furthermore, brands and their ad agencies may be so busy testing multimillion-dollar creative concepts that they neglect to ask consumers if advertising is even the right means by which to reach them.

Actually, says Schwartzapfel, "brands and their agencies can seek out consumer opinions until they are blue in the face and never discover what people actually care about. Or they can take the time to listen, because consumers are readily volunteering all sorts of facts about themselves." Furthermore, the information is largely unfettered, off the cuff, and without incentives, restrictions, moderation, or technology and marketing biases, which makes user generated content, comments, and conversations some of the best gauges for informing marketing strategies.

Conversation

How do you leverage listening to make better decisions?

Pete Blackshaw, global head of digital and social media, Nestlé: "The first thing I did when I got Nestlé was to develop a fairly comprehensive listening infrastructure that we were able to ramp up to about 40 markets in less than a year. That way, we put some discipline around listening to online conversations that could inform our business decisions. You measure earned media and can give debits and credits to certain marketing activities that are helping and hurting you. There are also very important tie-ins to the sales process, the supply chain process, corporate reputation, and market research applications."

Rikard Steiber, global marketing director, mobile and social advertising, Google: "On one hand, you need to be able to listen effectively to your fans and the people who are talking about your brand across different networks. Then, based on that, you need to be able to reach out to the right kind of audience with the right kind of message. And you need to be able to measure and get insights from the discussions regarding your return on investment and what you have learned, so you can do new things during your next campaign."

Andy Markowitz, director, global digital strategy, GE:
"Another way to get people engaged is to simply listen in the most basic way. And it doesn't cost anything. So we tell our businesses and their executives to sign up for Twitter and just listen. Listen to five people in your industry, five competitors, five peers, five thought leaders, to see what they say and what they point to. And then maybe one day they will feel comfortable enough to make a post and people may start to follow them. Just take it little by little by little."

Setting Standards

Unfortunately (and there always seems to be something unfortunate in these situations), many marketers are still not measuring their social strategies.[5] It is not that they don't recognize the value of analytics. To the contrary, research by social software company Bazaarvoice found that 82 percent of CMOs believe social data has a measurable effect on brand awareness.[6] In addition, more than 80 percent are at least "somewhat confident" that social initiatives have a measurable impact on brand loyalty. Rather, what is holding them back is the lack of a clear set of standards for what to measure and when.[7]

To that end, a strategy built on audience insights focuses on three critical components:

1. Success tracking and evaluation
2. Content optimization
3. Audience insight analysis

Success Tracking and Evaluation

For any brand in the social space, the basis for building its strategy, creating meaningful content, and getting that content to the right audiences is its capacity to understand its objectives fully. These goals serve as the criteria against which the brand gauges success.

The first step is to articulate what the brand wants to accomplish with its social media marketing efforts. It might include enhancing customer relationships through better engagement, increasing revenue, improving operations, or becoming the "go-to" source on issues that matter to its audience. Each objective must then be converted into a quantifiable metric that can be used to clearly define success. From there, the goals can be set for the key success metrics.

Once this groundwork has been established, the next component of every measurement plan involves tracking the key success metrics against the previous month, the previous year, and the previously defined goal. Such tracking provides the necessary context in which to determine whether the brand is achieving success at any given point. Monitoring such success trending also identifies peaks and troughs in the strategy, which will dictate how best to optimize content creation and distribution.

Content Optimization

At the core of any social strategy is the ability to manage relationships, whether they represent the connections between consumers and brands, consumers and consumers, or consumers and platforms or channels. As in any complex system, these various interactions overlap, and changes in one are sure to affect the others. It is particularly true of platforms, whose role in both the lives of consumers and the social strategy of brands constantly evolves.

Regularly monitoring interactions and engagement rates for each platform over time makes it possible to uncover better ways to use not only current popular platforms but also newcomers as well as platforms whose influence on success is declining. Because not all forms of engagement are equal, their rates are appropriately weighted. Likes are generally low rated because they are easy to achieve. Sharing, on the other hand, requires a greater commitment, thus scoring at the high end. Commenting falls somewhere in between.

For its part, content can be optimized by sorting it into relevant categories with similar subject matter. This step produces more discernible data sets that provide more reliable insights, which in turn lead to a greater increase in performance.

Furthermore, each piece of content can be grouped in multiple ways and applied to several different content analyses. A Facebook post, for example, can be classified as a "photo," as "nonbranded," and as "art." It can then be analyzed in the context of photos versus text only, branded versus nonbranded, and art versus lifestyle images. Such classification is the basis of every simple content analysis, although it is limited to determining the best content within a single category, independent of the other classes.

It is also possible, although less popular, to analyze content using statistics. In what is known as multivariate analysis, content is evaluated by identifying the most favorable combination of categories. Accordingly, the best Facebook post would be a photo that is also nonbranded and art. This so-called content recipe is used to drive a more sophisticated content strategy.

The principal advantage of optimization analysis is its ability to single out those parts of a strategy that work from those that do not. Nonetheless, optimization is by nature reductive, which means that the same successful pieces of a strategy will be implemented again and again, and tactics that fail to work will be abandoned. Over time, the number of options will continue to be reduced, which can become problematic.

Audience Insight Analysis

The solution is to perform an audience insight analysis, which is an expansive approach that identifies new tactics and opportunities using data available for each target audience. The objective is to examine an existing community as well as the aspirational target to gather intelligence about where members engage with social media, what their consumption habits are, and what they are talking about in the social sphere so as to design a comprehensive strategy.

Integrating these three components into a single structure ensures a deep understanding of current strategy performance and offers a comprehensive guide to increasing that performance in the future.

Keep in Mind . . .

1. In social media, one of the most important ways a brand can think is like its audience.
2. Even as more and more companies increase the amount of consumer data they collect, most still have a hard time making practical use of it.

(continued)

(Continued)

3. Traditional research and analytic techniques can be costly and time-consuming, and they can produce less than optimal results.
4. In the network model, research and analytics are combined with strategy development to create a more cost-effective and streamlined approach to audience insights.
5. The first step in the process is to identify a band's social marketing goals, after which appropriate metrics can be applied.
6. Regularly monitoring interactions and levels of engagement for each social channel makes it possible to discover more effective ways to use them.
7. Content can also be optimized by grouping and analyzing it in multiple ways.
8. Audience insight analysis is an expansive approach that identifies new tactics and opportunities using data available for each target audience.

Notes

1. Steve Mills, "Big Data: The New Natural Resource," *A Smarter Planet Blog*, March 20, 2012, http://asmarterplanet.com/blog/2012/03/big-data-the-new-natural-resource.html/.
2. "Marketers Find Less Than Half of Analytics Useful for Decision-Making," *eMarketer*, August 7, 2012, www.emarketer.com/Article.aspx?R=1009245&ecid=a6506033675d47f881651943c21c5ed4.
3. For example, people who are six months out from purchase are more passive and emotive in their online product research versus those who are one month out and are focusing on more tangible reasons for purchase, such as price and specific product benefits.
4. Doug Mataconis, "Polls That Include Cell Phones More Likely to Show Obama Leading," *Outside the Beltway*, September 22, 2012, www.outsidethebeltway.com/polls-that-include-cell-phones-more-likely-to-show-obama-leading/.
5. "2012 Social Media Marketing Industry Report," *Social Media Examiner*, April 2012, www.socialmediaexaminer.com/SocialMediaMarketingIndustryReport2012.pdf.
6. "Social Trends Report 2012," *Bazaarvoice*, June 4, 2012, www.bazaarvoice.com/social-trends-report-2012.
7. "2012 Social Media Marketing Industry Report."

CHAPTER 14

The Art and Science of Listening

E ffective listening is both an art and a science. That is why the network model employs leading edge systems and technology to pinpoint audiences' needs, wants, interests, and attitudes. This approach focuses on three key variables (Figure 14.1).

1. The **business mandate** is those brand objectives that need to be addressed through social programs.
2. **Audience truths** define each target group in a social sphere according to where they are, what they do there, how they feel, and what they want.
3. **Brand truths** determine how much a brand's products or services are acknowledged and appreciated across the competitive landscape.

When dealing with social media, many marketers have a good idea of what their brand objectives are and what they hope to achieve. It is in the process of achieving those goals that they often run into trouble. One way to improve the odds is to review, and possibly refine, the mandates by thoroughly examining their entire inventory of marketing resources. Included here are all promotional materials, whether or not they are successful; endorsement deals; licensing agreements; existing media; creative properties; and social media activities. It is also a good idea to

Figure 14.1   Three Key Data Sets

reach across a brand's enterprise—and beyond—to question assumptions, broaden perspectives, and further clarify objectives.

At that point, the focus shifts to the audience, and the challenge for marketers is to be able to see them the way they see themselves. An effective technique is by using two distinct types of research: platform-level analysis and social listening. In platform-level analysis, every piece of content on every channel in a brand's network is thoroughly scrutinized to determine exactly how consumers engage with it, including their rates of likes, comments, and sharing. Each of these engagements is then analyzed on a platform level to gauge how it performs within the social landscape and to judge how well a brand is connecting with consumers relative to its competitors.

Social Personas

These days, of course, the number of channels and platforms keeps expanding, as does the multitude of people using them, making it that much more difficult to effectively define audiences. Regardless of these circumstances, segmentation remains a staple part of marketing due diligence by distinguishing subsets of customers—or prospective customers—who share common characteristics within particular markets.

In more traditional marketing circles, segmentation formats usually draw on demographics, but that is starting to change as companies recognize the limitations of scoring consumers according to customary descriptors like age, income, and gender. One of the first brands to move in a new direction was NBC News, whose digital division turned its attention to consumer behaviors or personas, dividing its audience by how passionately they engaged with the news.[1] As a result, NBC has been able to not only change its digital news product, but also design its advertising to better align with its editorial content.

Social marketing, too, has its share of personas, and these familiar personalities are evaluated on an ongoing basis to distill both targeting and retargeting efforts. Rather than rely on consumers to volunteer information about their interests and behaviors through incentivized panels or surveys that can sometimes be inaccurate, however, social marketers value a very different currency on which to base their decisions: conversation.

Listening Tools

Conversation is crucial because social media marketing is essentially about enhancing existing behaviors, not creating new ones. To accurately determine what content to develop and how best to deploy it, brands must first understand what audiences are talking about, as well as why, where, and how they are doing so. Hence, in the same way that companies segment consumers based on self-described preferences or stated frequency of purchase, they can dissect conversations so as to enable brand managers to distinguish the kinds of information and ideas that motivate dialogue across target markets.

Social segmentation and personas are still as much the products of critical evaluation as they are the results of scientific study, and both the art and science of listening are fluid. After all, no two conversations are exactly the same, so no two markets can be segmented and defined in the same way. Nonetheless, the power and sophistication of advanced listening tools make it possible to systematically scrub for just about anything a creative and strategically inclined mind can dream up, and with remarkable precision and quality.

For example, within 48 hours of the release of the iPhone 5, social media research firm Crimson Hexagon had gathered and analyzed more than 1.5 million tweets about the highly anticipated smartphone.[2] Using technology developed at Harvard University, it was able to discern both the substance and sentiment of the comments. Moreover, the company offered a feature that allowed end users to dynamically train its listening engine to make appropriate sentiment decisions over time, autonomously selecting which tweets to pick up and which to ignore.

That is only an inkling of what powerful listening tools can achieve. Even long-established systems, such as Boolean logic, are being retooled for the twenty-first century. First conceived more than 150 years ago, Boolean language has become a standard for digital search by combining words and phrases into statements that can retrieve documents from searchable databases anywhere in the world. Now it is being combined with robust web crawlers and platform feeds to generate ever more meaningful conversational insights, trends, and campaign performance benchmarks. Consequently, social analytics companies such as Sysomos offer the means to monitor myriad conversations to extract the most relevant mentions and create real-time accounts of how people, products, and brands are covered across social media sites.

Audience Truths Are Brand Truths

Social segmentation and personas are at the heart of audience truths, and unlike their more traditional counterparts, they are designed to comfortably place brands into existing conversations instead of interrupting or intruding on them. Even so, several fundamental criteria must be met to ensure that segmentation is a success:

- **Is the segment inherently social?** There are few, if any, segments of the population that social media marketing does not touch, but some are certainly more socially active than others. So, it is vital that the choice clearly reflects a brand's mandates.
- **What types of content does the target audience react to?** Social content takes on many forms, all of which are designed to elicit dialogue users. Photos, videos, status updates, check-ins, and so forth are all fair game when considering how best to segment by content type.
- **Is the segment accessible?** How well a brand's mandate coincides with a particular audience's truths will determine its segment fit and how often it is mentioned in conversation.
- **Is the segment measurable?** If there is enough realistic, scalable engagement and topic data to properly consider segment growth potential, it is possible to segment by conversation volume or some such metric.

The right answers to these questions don't provide the kinds of big data that have become the holy grail of marketing, but they do offer simple and intuitive insights that ultimately inform brand truths. They represent consumer opinions, beliefs, and behaviors that define the relationships between brands and their audiences, and they have the potential to alter brand mandates as well.

The Engagement Point

Business mandates, audience truths, and brand truths are integral to every social media marketing strategy. Individually, they reveal valuable internal and external intelligence. Together, they provide a single organizing principle for meaningful engagement. Thus, it is critical to find the sweet spot where these three constituents overlap (Figure 14.2). This spot is the engagement point, and it affirms audience truths by zeroing in on how consumers use and respond to social media content. At the same time, it ratifies brand truths by acknowledging what a brand stands for and how it is perceived in the marketplace. Plus, it continually aligns both with a brand's yearlong business goals.

Rather than a set of static, interlocking circles, however, audience truths, brand truths, and the business mandate are more like three separate wheels of fortune, each spinning in different directions and at varying speeds; thus, the engagement point can change as circumstances within each circle changes. Moreover, the entire process is nonlinear (Figure 14.3). Every decision that is made and every action that is taken can result in new insights or outcomes that can loop back and possibly alter the strategy.

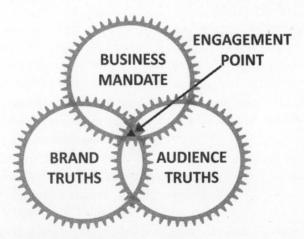

Figure 14.2 Finding the Engagement Point

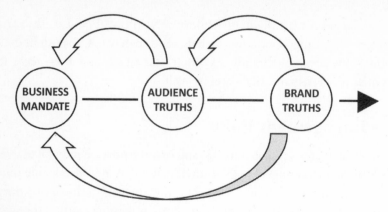

Figure 14.3   Driving Insights

On one hand, the engagement point sets the conditions for successful campaigns that audiences can grab on to while also serving the needs of brands. On the other hand, by prescribing the parameters and proof points that define initiatives across a variety of social channels, it provides guidance for those on the network team who are charged with developing creative content.

The engagement point is more than just a crossroad or launch pad, though. Above all else, it encompasses the special qualities around which to build a brand's social identity. This unique identity gives the brand a validated platform by which to connect with audiences through relevant content and memorable social experiences.

Consistent Conversations

One way to ensure good experiences is through consistent and compelling conversations. The world of social media is inherently content driven, and, by extension, so are the myriad conversations that reside there. Regularly creating content that engages the same audiences again and again engenders ongoing interactions, whether between brands and consumers or among consumers themselves. It also leads consumers to expect certain kinds of user experiences. By promoting consistent conversations and fulfilling expectations, brands share priorities with their audiences. Initially, they address consumers' needs and interests by providing relevant information. From there, they reach in and touch emotions, which is the primary driver of sharing.

Although most denizens of social networks are adept at creating and carrying on conversations, there are often opportunities to energize them. In such situations, tent poles serve two purposes. First, they can be used to start new conversations by introducing a product or service or by coordinating with a special event. Whatever a tent pole represents, it must jibe with the current conversation before it is placed on the grid.

Second, tent poles can enhance existing conversations at points where their intensity is abating by creating content that supplements a brand's media inventory. This step can dramatically spread a brand's social message to additional participants.

At the heart of every conversation, though, should be the very notion of being social. A conversation is not merely a creative solution. It is a creative *social* solution. Therefore, it should not only be driven by a brand's content, but also by the content created by its audience. That is what makes it a genuine exchange of ideas, experiences, and passions. Without that, there is no give-and-take. There is no engagement.

Keep in Mind . . .

1. In the network model, every successful listening strategy takes into account three key variables: a brand's objectives (business mandate), the audiences' interests and desires (audience truths), and how a brand's products and services are perceived (brand truths).
2. This approach employs two separate forms of research: platform-level analysis, which scrutinizes every channel in a brand's network; and social listening, which continually monitors all conversations.
3. Social personas are determined by how consumers engage with a brand across channels and platforms.
4. Brands have access to an increasing number of tools that enable them to carefully listen to and thoroughly analyze social conversations.
5. The engagement point is the sweet spot where business mandates, audience truths, and brand truths come together to define relationships between brands and their audiences.
6. By consistently creating content that fulfills consumer expectations, brands share priorities with their audiences.

Notes

1. Joe Mandese, "NBC News Kills the Demographic, Personifies Its Viewers Instead," *Online Media Daily*, October 3, 2012, www.mediapost.com/publications/article/184424/nbc-news-kills-the-demographic-personifies-its-vi.html.
2. Philip Elmer-DeWitt, "What Twitter Had to Say about Apple's iPhone 5 Event," *CNNMoney*, September 13, 2012, http://tech.fortune.cnn.com/2012/09/13/what-twitter-had-to-say-about-apples-iphone-5-event/.

SECTION IV

Content Is Currency

CHAPTER 15

Content at the Speed of Culture

I n the summer of 2012, as a fierce copyright battle between Apple and Samsung raged on and not long before the introduction of the much anticipated iPhone 5, rumors began to surface about a new asymmetric screw Apple had developed that would make it more difficult for hackers to open and explore the inner workings of its products. Word of the device first appeared on social news site reddit, which included a three-dimensional mockup of the protective piece of hardware (Figure 15.1). Within 12 hours, stories began to show up on Yahoo!, *Macworld*, and *Wired* along with a video on YouTube.

The screw itself never materialized. That is because Day4, a now-defunct motion graphics company out of Stockholm, Sweden, had posted the information as a hoax to see how rumors spread online.[1] Because Apple has a strict policy about keeping its product plans secret, the company made no attempt to respond, but that didn't stop Apple watchers. Although some tech journalists had reservations about the authenticity of the report, many commentators ran with it, as did the social communities. According to Day4 spokesperson at the time, Lukasz Lindell, "On Twitter, numerous posts raged about the issue. On YouTube, people made video blogs about the new screw. Google+ talked about it page after page" (Figure 15.2). Lindell later apologized for the prank, but had the intent been more malicious, it could have turned into a nasty crisis.

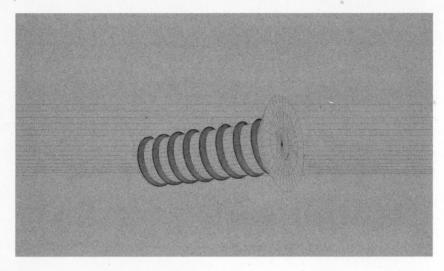

Figure 15.1   Hardware Mockup

Figure 15.2   Twitter Conversation

Internet Time on Steroids

Nearly 20 years ago, someone coined the term *Internet time* to underscore the perception that the speed of almost all forms of content seems to accelerate online. It was based on the premise that the efficiency of digital technologies made it possible to move information faster, more easily, and more quickly to just about any point on the globe. Since then, the process has been significantly hastened by social media. Indeed, it took more than 50 years for the telephone to reach critical mass. TV shortened that time considerably to just 13 years; in the 5 years after the Internet began carrying commercial traffic, service providers signed up more than 50 million subscribers. Facebook reached 50 million users a mere year after Mark Zuckerberg opened it to the public, and Twitter did the same in just nine months.[2]

The speed at which content can be produced and distributed has radically altered almost all types of business processes, especially marketing, but even though information increasingly travels at the speed of digits, the human capacity to understand much of it still moves at the speed of atoms. In many instances, the time available to respond to an event after it has occurred effectively has all but vanished, ratcheting up the pressure on organizations vying for the public's attention to make rash and sometimes flawed decisions. For example, minutes after the Supreme Court released its historic ruling on the Affordable Care Act, CNN, in an attempt to get the jump on its competitors, declared on its website that the court had "struck down [the] individual mandate for health care." A similar tweet quickly followed (Figure 15.3).

The problem was that CNN had gotten it completely wrong, and in its later correction, noted:

In his opinion, Chief Justice Roberts initially said that the individual mandate was not a valid exercise of Congressional power under the Commerce Clause. CNN reported that fact, but then wrongly reported

Figure 15.3   Twitter Conversation

that therefore the court struck down the mandate as unconstitutional. However, that was not the whole of the Court's ruling. CNN regrets that it didn't wait to report out the full and complete opinion regarding the mandate. We made a correction within a few minutes and apologize for the error.

Caught Short

Apologies like these are becoming seemingly routine. To be fair, CNN was not the only news organization to get it wrong. NPR had tweeted similar misinformation moments earlier, and Fox was not far behind. At least three members of Congress also tweeted erroneously. Nonetheless, although online speed may not kill, it can certainly do damage. The embarrassment may have been greatest for CNN, whose only competitive advantage over MSNBC and Fox News is that most viewers rely on it for coverage of breaking news.

Still, news networks are hardly the only brands struggling to keep pace with the speed of today's culture, and the problem is particularly acute for those that have been targets of social media assaults. According to a study by Ethical Corporation, an independent business intelligence firm, one in five companies that have been subject to social media criticism are completely unprepared to deal with it.[3] Similar research by Altimeter Group found that the majority of businesses lack the appropriate internal education, the proper professional staff, and a well-defined social media policy.[4]

Conversation

How does the pace of social media change marketing strategy?

Jason Hirschhorn, owner, ReDEF Group: "Remember how it used to be? You stood outside to buy Pearl Jam at 12:00 a.m. at Tower Records. Then you went home with the physical CD and listened to the album; after which you would probably call up a friend—or see them later in the week—and say, 'You've got to hear this song "Dissident," you'll love it.' Nowadays, I can have that same conversation immediately."

Sharon Feder, chief operating officer, Mashable: "A few years ago, brands needed to have a website and some level of customer service. And now there is really this almost requirement that brands are always on, always accessible to their consumers or their community."

Reggie Bradford, senior vice president of product development, Oracle: "This is a very perishable medium, in the sense that things happen on a global basis all the time in their real time, whether it's a crisis in the Middle East or an election or a hurricane, and those brands that can truly humanize and create and engage in those conversations in real time are obviously more effective and become part of that dialogue with those consumers."

Ted Rubin, chief social marketing officer, Collective Bias: "I see all too many brands that finally make a commitment and say they are going to be there and build the brand strategy. But then they take months to come up with what their message is going to be. So they stay stuck on the message instead of realizing that every community evolves and has to be fluid."

Andy Markowitz, director, global digital strategy, GE: "From a social perspective and the need for engagement, you can't have stale content up there, because anything longer than several hours is like Dead Sea Scrolls."

Faster Equals More

The faster and easier it is to generate content, the more it becomes available. It is estimated that 600 new blog posts are published every minute and 30,000 tweets are created every minute.[5] As noted previously, however, those blogs and tweets are still considerably fewer than the 30 billion pieces of content posted on average on Facebook every 30 days. Add the vast trail of information left by online ads, searches, and smartphone use—plus the ever more ubiquitous "Internet of things" that does not even require human interaction—and now we need a new lexicon to calculate it all, with terms like gigabyte, petabyte, zettabyte, and most recently yottabyte, which is designated by the number 1 followed by 24 zeroes.

Sometimes the problem it is not just a matter of how fast information appears, but also how quickly it can disappear. For example, the average commercial content posted on a Facebook page has a shelf life of barely 18 hours.[6] Such a life span may even be more abbreviated on Twitter. Visualizing the content can help. Photographs tend to prolong shelf life by about 9 percent, and video can extend it as much as 16 percent.

Inundated by so much data coming at them in different formats, at breakneck speed, consumers are seeking the means to cope with it all. One of the most popular techniques is multitasking, but it is also proving to be among the least effective. Ample evidence that multitasking, like the glut of information itself, results in diminished creativity and poor decisions.[7] In fact, only about 2 percent of multitaskers do so successfully.[8]

Another option is the inclination to personalize content choices. Whether on their own or with the help of sophisticated third-party algorithms that select content based on users' past experiences, consumers are consolidating their sources of information. Although that helps them make sense of their worlds, it can also construct walls that isolate them and create so-called echo chambers, which makes it harder for brands to reach them with new or different ideas.

Despite the apparently staggering amount of content being created and consumed, not everyone is beset by the abundance. A study out of Northwestern University found that "very few Americans seem to feel bogged down or overwhelmed by the volume of news and information at their fingertips and on their screens."[9] Among those who do are consumers who haven't yet mastered social media filters and search engine navigation.

A Matter of Control

Perhaps it is just a question of time until brands and marketers catch up, but the current big three forces in the digital world—social media, big data, and cloud computing—will continue to increase the amount of available information and the speed at which it arrives. So, the challenge will be to learn how to master both the amount and speed of information, even as they continue to expand.

Clearly, brands need to take advantage of real-time conversations to successfully participate in social media, and they must modify their business models in terms of how long it takes them to create content, approve it, and get it out the door. Doing so means being able to step back and scan all the critical components—ideas, issues, audiences, and technologies—and observing how the different pieces interact and influence one another. It also means giving up some control.

Accepting the lack of control is a critical part of social strategy, and it is one many brands find hard to swallow. After all, they have spent generations putting processes and provisions in place to govern as much of the purchasing funnel as possible, carefully creating just about everything that goes into the marketplace. "Now they are being told that they are going to have to invite consumers to participate," says Big Fuel's managing director Christine Shoaf. "Not just to watch, but to express their opinions . . . publicly."

The types of controls that have enabled brands to master past arts of marketing are becoming impediments to building lasting relationships with consumers. Like so much else in a constantly changing social ecosphere, they must also come to realize that control can be an illusion.

Instagram found that out at the end of 2012, when the Facebook-owned photo-sharing service updated its terms of service to give itself the perpetual right to sell its users' photographs without payment or notification. Not surprisingly, the decision was met with much protest. The company quickly backpedaled as chief executive officer Kevin Systrom blogged "Because of the feedback we have heard from you, we are reverting this advertising section to the original version that has been in effect since we launched the service in October 2010."[10] Unfortunately for Systrom, the apology did not prevent a class-action lawsuit.

Conversation

Can brands continue to maintain control over their message and still develop strong relationships with consumers?

Jason Hirschhorn, owner, ReDEF Group: "To think that you could avoid social, even if you don't participate in it—which would be insanity—is impossible. Meaning, in this day and age, you don't have full control over your brand. You may think you do. You may be the CMO of the company, you may be the brand manager, but you do not have complete control, because

(continued)

(*Continued*)

anyone can say anything, share anything, discuss anything, comment on anything having to do with your brand online."

Herb Scannell, president, BBC Worldwide America at BBC Worldwide: "Some brands are afraid of what their fans can do; but they have to get over it and figure out how they can harness it to some end, while also being ready and willing to take on the thorny stuff that comes with fans."

Sharon Feder, chief operating officer, Mashable: "At the end of the day, brands need to be able to make the transition; to be able to take a step back from the ad copy that they are committed to and allow content that takes into account not just those brand values they are trying to communicate, but also allows consumers to interact about something that is of interest to them."

Scannell: "Companies also have many employees at their disposal who should be able to communicate as brand advocates. If your employees don't like your products, who is going to like them? If you are afraid of what your employees are going to say, you have the wrong employees."

Keep in Mind . . .

1. Whereas it took nearly a lifetime for the telephone and more than a decade for TV to reach critical mass, Twitter did so in less than a year.
2. In their attempt to keep up with rapidly developing events, brands may actually contribute to the amount of misinformation online.
3. Despite their increased use of social and digital media, many organizations are still unprepared to handle possible crises that may result.
4. Content online can vanish as quickly as it appears, although visual material such as photographs and video can help prolong its life span.
5. Multitasking and personalization are two ways consumers are trying to cope with ever-expanding amounts of information.
6. To successfully reach consumers and build strong relationships through social channels, brands must learn to relinquish control over many types of interactions.

Notes

1. Lukasz Lindell, "How We Screwed (Almost) the Whole Apple Community," *Day4 Blogg*, August 13, 2012, http://day4.se/how-we-screwed-almost-the-whole-apple-community/.

2. Jacques Bughin, Michael Chui, and James Manyika, "Capturing Business Value with Social Technology," *McKinsey Quarterly*, November 2012, https://www.mckinsey-quarterly.com/Strategy/Growth/Capturing_business_value_with_social_technologies_3029.

3. Ethical Corporation, "Communications, Campaigns and Social Media: How Companies Respond to Consumers and Activists in a Crisis," July 2012, http://events.ethicalcorp.com/documents/Crisis_Comms_Findings.pdf.

4. Altimeter Group, "Social Business Readiness: How Advanced Companies Prepare Internally," August 31, 2011, www.slideshare.net/jeremiah_owyang/social-readiness-how-advanced-companies-prepare.

5. Steve Mills, "Big Data: The New Natural Resource," *A Smarter Planet Blog*, March 20, 2012, http://asmarterplanet.com/blog/2012/03/big-data-the-new-natural-resource.html.

6. Steve McClellan, "Marketing Content Has Short Shelf Life On Facebook," *Online Media Daily*, June 28, 2012, www.mediapost.com/publications/article/177831/marketing-content-has-short-shelf-life-on-facebook.html.

7. Jim Taylor, "Technology: Myth of Multitasking," *Psychology Today*, March 30, 2011, www.psychologytoday.com/blog/the-power-prime/201103/technology-myth-multitasking.

8. Matt Petrozonio, "Only 2% of People Can Multitask Successfully," *Mashable*, August 13, 2012, http://mashable.com/2012/08/13/multitasking-infographic/.

9. Erin White, "Information Overload?" Northwestern University, August 30, 2012, www.northwestern.edu/newscenter/stories/2012/08/hargittai-info-overload.html.

10. Kevin Systrom, "Updated Terms of Service Based on Your Feedback," Instagram, December 20, 2012, http://blog.instagram.com/post/38421250999/updated-terms-of-service-based-on-your-feedback.

CHAPTER 16

Content That Connects

Product stories appeal to brands, but people stories attract and engage their audiences. For anyone who works in social media—or simply participates in it—that seems like a no-brainer, but as earlier chapters have already demonstrated, a great many brands still don't get it. According to research by IBM's Institute for Business Value, nearly three-quarters of executives surveyed in 2011 believe the primary reason consumers follow their companies across social media is to learn about new products (see Figure 16.1).[1] Yet barely 50 percent of consumers agree with that notion. Even fewer feel closely connected to the brands with which they interact.

At the very least, successful social content must be something that an audience—not a brand—needs or wants. It can run the gamut from primarily utilitarian to purely entertaining (Figure 16.2), but it has to have some perceived value before consumers will engage with it. If the content can evoke an emotion, it is not just viewable, but also sharable. Brands that create sharable content benefit from having consumers talking to other consumers about their product or services rather than having to do it themselves.

Design for Social Media

At one time, a brand only had to be concerned with one online presence, its website. A classic form of owned media, the website was often where potential customers spent most of their time interfacing with the brand, forming first impressions, and making purchasing decisions. More

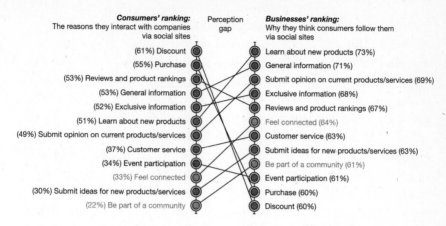

Figure 16.1 Perception Gap between Brands and Consumers

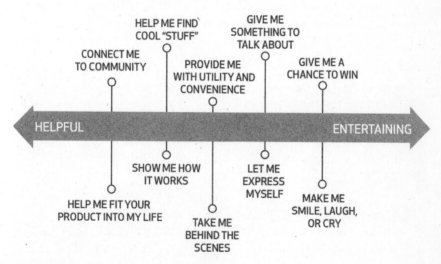

Figure 16.2 The Content Spectrum

recently, however, that piece of digital property has had to compete with an entire social ecosystem for consumers' time and attention; where a company once needed to manage a single online presence, it now has scores of others that must be designed, built, and maintained.

If it were just a matter of doing that on one piece of digital real estate—say, the desktop—it would be challenging enough, but brands must connect with consumers across a varied landscape of big, small, fixed, and mobile platforms, each with its own unique user experiences. At one end of the spectrum, an expanding number of consumers are watching web videos on large, plasma-screen televisions,[2] either through Internet-connected sets or devices like video game consoles or streaming media players. At the other end, the percentage of mobile subscribers watching video on their phones has increased significantly.[3]

In addition, the popularity of sites such as Pinterest and Instagram underscore the need for brands to embrace the growing trend of visual storytelling. Content on these platforms elicit strong emotions among their audiences. A 2012 study by ROI Research found that when users connect with friends on social media, it is the pictures they post that are enjoyed the most.[4] More than 4 out of 10 respondents also said they are more likely to engage with brands that post pictures than those that provide information in any other medium. Joint research by communications agency M Booth and analytics firm SimplyMeasure also determined that photos are shared twice as much, and videos 12 times as much, as text updates.[5] In fact, photo and video posts on Pinterest alone refer more traffic than Twitter, StumbleUpon, Google+, or LinkedIn.

Conversation

As visual imagery and video become more popular online, how can social marketers tap into these resources to make their content more compelling?

Dylan Edgar, vice president, content production, Big Fuel: "What we have done in video production is take the same work ethic as in high-quality television and brought it to agency space. It is a different deliverable in a shorter form, but the production value is comparable because the equipment is good enough to match broadcast quality content online. That is important, since online is becoming the new broadcast channel. But it is that production work ethic—how you can do more with less; how you can turn around faster; how you can tell compelling human stories—that is most important."

Sharon Feder, chief operating officer, Mashable: "The visual experience and the necessity of creating great assets that can translate on any device is going to be incredibly important.

I think the requirements for content creators are to be able to attract audiences to their content and tell stories using visuals. One of the things that I see is what GE is doing with visuals on Facebook. I see them as a great example of a brand that's really getting it and really growing their brand reputation as a result as a brand that really plays well in social.

Andy Markowitz, Director, global digital strategy, GE: "The content [at GE] that really works well and gets a lot of engagement [is] the kind of video and pictures that make us look cool. So if you look at our website, we do quick flyovers over our factories and you can see the technology that is at play. Content like 'Stump the Scientist,' where audiences can submit questions to our global research team on any topic that sparks their interest or ignites their curiosity. That kind of content that gives people a peek into who we are. And we hear, over and over again, words like 'credibility' and 'authenticity' about what we do."

Interactive Technology for Social

The advancement of media, by which an emerging system alters or replaces its predecessor, is unstoppable, but at no other time in history has it appeared to be as rapid or as radical as it is today. Technologies, trends, and user behaviors are all changing seemingly at once, and keeping up with them both separately and collectively is paramount to creating successful online experiences.

Just as important is the ability to deliver those experiences across a range of devices, including interactive television, personal computers, consoles, tablets, and smartphones. Thinking multiplatform is no longer optional. Because making branded experiences readily accessible to users results in much higher rates of satisfaction, it is mandatory. There are four key factors of multiplatform thinking:

1. Responsive designs that address the specific device being used while maintaining a consistent experience across all platforms
2. Programming frameworks that allow for rapid prototyping to quickly capitalize on new opportunities and trends
3. Hosting that is intended to handle ever-heavier loads as more content goes viral

4. Experimentation that leverages standards at the very moment they cross the threshold of user adoption to provide never-before-seen interactive experiences

Video for Social Media

Of all forms of online content, none is more popular today than video, which is fast becoming the standard medium of the online world. More than 85 percent of U.S. brand and agency marketers polled in 2012 by content discovery platform Outbrain have created video for content marketing.[6] For their part, 9 out of 10 U.S. consumers view videos online in some form.[7] During the month of August 2012 alone, Americans averaged more than seven hours streaming and watching more than 27 billion video programs.[8] Video's popularity is not only limited to viewing. In a study of the top 10 brands on Facebook, users shared videos 12 times more than photos and text posts combined.[9]

Not surprisingly, successfully producing and delivering video must be an essential component of every brand's content portfolio. For video to be effective, however, and especially for it to gain traction on social channels, it must abide by the best practices of the medium. For example, conventional brand videos are product focused, with the intent of informing passive viewers; social videos must be people focused, with the goal of promoting engagement and sharing. In broadcast media, commercial content is an interruption, but in social media, it risks being an unwanted intrusion if carelessly inserted into consumer conversations. Rather than encroach on the experience, it has to *be* the experience; otherwise, it is going to have few views, poor share rates, and ultimately require the support of paid media to reach its desired audience.

It is possible to engage an audience with content that is entertaining, amusing, sometimes amazing, informative, or enlightening, but sharing only happens when engaged audiences are also deeply moved by what they encounter. Although it is difficult to quantify exactly what arouses audiences, there are several general goals video must achieve:

- Elicit an emotional response as soon as possible within the video because drop-off will occur within as little as 10 to 15 seconds if a viewer does not quickly connect with the content.

- Maintain the emotional connection throughout the video by continually building on the initial response.
- Make it easy for the audience to share the content by providing the means to:
  - Put it on YouTube, which, as the number-two search engine in the world, is still the optimal destination for social video sharing.
  - Make the video embeddable so that viewers can post it to their own social network feeds.
  - Allow audience to "like" it and comment on it.
- Avoid heavily branding video content because that is viewed as an interruption akin to traditional commercials; organically include the brand when and where appropriate.

Moreover, certain types of social videos work better than others:

- **Memes:** Internet inside jokes (i.e., cats, demotivational posters) and hyperrelevant topics
- **News:** Information that people are actively looking to consume and that takes advantage of video search engine optimization
- **How-To and DIY:** Education around passion points
- **Music:** Performances and parodies
- **Stunts:** Real or staged, but which produce some form of shock value or amazement

Whatever the approach, it is critical that the social videos tell compelling stories that go beyond traditional marketing or public relations tactics, in ways that are both professional and practical.

Development and Production Slates

Audience insights that combine a comprehensive strategy with intelligible analytics make it possible to genuinely understand consumers. From that point on, however, it is all about creating compelling content. Although all the above techniques work toward that end, keeping an audience truly engaged over time requires a robust and relevant content strategy. For that reason, innovative development and production are crucial to social marketing.

Development and production teams are responsible for the kinds of content that inspire the network model and fuel consumer conversations. This content usually takes one of two forms: a conversation may start out socially as a blog, tweet, Facebook post, or image on Pinterest or Instagram, or it may originate outside the social sphere. Super Bowl commercials, for example, are as eagerly anticipated as the game itself. Consumers—even those who have little or no interest in football—can preview the ads before the first kickoff and generate considerable buzz around particular brands, thus amplifying the marketing opportunity.

Within the network model, the content development team is charged with conceptualizing creative ideas and then selling them to whomever foots the bill. It may be in response to a specific proposal request, as part of a big pitch to a client or senior executive, or as the next stage of an ongoing campaign. If there is buy-in, the content production team then takes on the concept and turns it into something that will appeal to target audiences.

Because there are two different stages in the course of creating content—development and production—it is necessary to manage the entire process so that it is apparently seamless. Accordingly, both teams maintain slates that serve as organizational tools to keep track of all activities.

The content development slate is designed to oversee various pitches and existing concepts. It enables the content development team to recognize a brand's voice, put together a program that meets expressed needs, and deliver it as planned. One way to think of content development is as a general practitioner who diagnoses a patient's overall health and then directs him to the appropriate specialists, who in this case would be the production teams.

Because various teams may simultaneously work on multiple deliverables—particularly if the individual deliverables are part of a larger whole—there must be some method to monitor their progress. Establishing a production slate provides a way to identify what is "in production" and how far along it is on a timeline. If such projects are also being carried out across different production disciplines—including design, interactive technology, and video—a slate is crucial.

Slates may vary from brand to brand or strategy to strategy, but at a bare minimum they include information regarding the brand, the project name, every stage of production, calendar milestones, and the owners of the project or stages. Despite their separate areas of focus, content development and production slates are not mutually exclusive. While the content development team usually oversees the pitch process, it may draw on production resources when needed. On the flip side, a content development slate may also have oversight for guaranteeing that what was sold is actually delivered. Even though content development is not directly involved in producing specific content, it is responsible for ensuring that the end product is the same as what was originally pitched, and this team works closely with production across all disciplines and platforms. "There are always checks and balances," says Dylan Edgar, director of content production at Big Fuel, "and when we work like that, we work best."

Keep in Mind . . .

1. As consumers move easily from one form of media to another, content must be developed and produced for a broad range of channels and platforms.
2. Today, every brand's content portfolio must include video, with the expectation that it will not only be viewed, but also very likely shared.
3. Successful social content requires both innovative content development and imaginative production services.
4. The content development team is responsible for conceptualizing creative ideas and oversees all projects by way of a development slate.
5. The content production team takes the concept and transforms it into something engaging, using a production slate to identify the status of everything that is "in production."

Notes

1. IBM Institute for Business Value, "From Social Media to Social CRM: What Customers Want," IBM, February 2011, http://public.dhe.ibm.com/common/ssi/ecm/en/gbe03391usen/GBE03391USEN.PDF.

2. According to research by the NPD Group, 45 percent of people surveyed say that the TV is their "primary screen" for watching paid and free videos streamed over the Internet. Peter Kafka, "Tipping Point? We're Watching More Web Video on TVs Than on PCs," *All Things Digital*, September 26, 2012, http://allthingsd.com/20120926/tipping-point-were-watching-more-web-video-on-tvs-than-pcs/.

3. According to the Nielsen Company, the number of subscribers who view video on their phones grew by more than 25 percent in 2011. Nielsen Company, "The Cross-Platform Report: How and Where Content Is Watched." Quarter 1, 2012, www.nielsen.com/content/dam/corporate/us/en/reports-downloads/2012-Reports/Nielsen-Cross-Platform-Report-Q1-2012-final.pdf.

4. ROI Research, "Life On Demand: Participant Behavior and Social Engagement," *Slideshare*, July 25, 2012, www.slideshare.net/performics_us/performics-life-on-demand-2012-summary-deck.

5. Stephanie Buck, "For Brand Engagement, Visuals Rule," *Mashable*, August 24, 2012, http://mashable.com/2012/08/24/visual-storytelling-brands/.

6. "Marketers Deploy, Measure 'Non-Promotional' Content," *eMarketer*, October 23, 2012, www.emarketer.com/%28S%28gjrgkh45dmewndatycqrprnz%29%29/Article.aspx?R=1009432.

7. "Video for SEO: 90 Percent of Consumers Watch Video Online, Search Drives Discovery," *Brafton*, October 17, 2012, www.brafton.com/news/video-for-seo-90-percent-of-consumers-watch-video-online-search-drives-discovery.

8. Nielsen Company, "August 2012: Top Online Video Sites," *Nielsen Wire*, September 27, 2012, http://blog.nielsen.com/nielsenwire/online_mobile/august-2012-top-u-s-video-sites/.

9. Kristin Piombino, "Photos and Video Drive Most Engagement on Social Media," *Ragan.com*, September 5, 2012, www.ragan.com/Main/Articles/4a910fff-3b4d-44e5-a650-3e161a3f674c.aspx.

CHAPTER 17

The Creative Process

When building a creative program in the social space, many considerations should be taken into account. For example, exactly who is the audience, and how do they acquire, perceive, interpret, decide, and act on information? Moreover, how do they use and interact with an ever-expanding range of platforms and channels? Probably no factor is more significant than the ability to arouse the strongest possible emotional response from the end user. That is because emotionally charged content is better remembered than neutral content, and it can be recalled with greater accuracy.[1] Most important, it is also most likely to be shared.

Content that elicits emotions does so because it connects an audience to other people, places, or events. It helps them determine how they feel about the world. It defines their experiences and drives their behavior, sometimes unconsciously.[2] Therefore, in the context of the network model, succeeding in social media means being able to fuel those multiple elements. What is more, content must continually change to stay fresh and be worthy of conversation. One of the most effective ways to do so is through powerful campaigns, which are creative concepts designed to propel the overall network goal forward.

Building a Franchise

The best social campaigns can be thought of as franchises in much the same way as TV series are. In both instances, franchises generate considerable interest and loyalty, and they often serve as the topics of water cooler conversations. In addition, they can readily cross over from one medium or channel to another. It is not unusual for a TV series, for example, to have originated in another medium, as with the recurrent depictions of Superman over the years, or to have spawned its own film franchises, such as the *Star Trek* phenomenon. That way, the relationships franchises build with their audiences are continuous and long term.

In the case of social campaigns, long-term continuity comes from linking campaigns to the appropriate business solutions within a brand's network. Once one or more solutions have been identified, the content development team can come up with the creative programs to layer on top of them. Simply aligning with business solutions doesn't automatically achieve continuity, however. To maintain ongoing conversations with their audiences, brands must develop a reliable strategy and establish both a consistent tone of voice and creative approach.

Campaigns Come in Two Parts

Creating a successful campaign generally consists of two overlapping processes: developing compelling content and determining how people will discover it. What constitutes quality content is the ability to capture an audience's attention, pique their interest, and stir their emotions. Ideally, it should also do so across more than one business solution. In a complex social media ecosystem, brands must be prepared to tell their stories across ever-changing permutations of channels, platforms, media, and solutions, giving their audiences multiple options about how to access and engage.

The probability that audiences will share content is proportionately related to their level of exposure. The more they are exposed to particular content, the more likely they are to share it, provided it meets all the aforementioned creative criteria and provided the brand has established a unified creative position that audiences encounter as they move throughout the social web.

Target Audiences

Within the context of the network model and in accordance with the grid, it is also important that campaigns target specific audiences. Throughout much of social media's history, people and the virtual communities where they reside have been defined in terms of social graphs based on shared personal connections. Increasingly, however, online populations are also interacting via interest graphs, which bring together persons whose only bond may be their mutual concerns and curiosities. Here, too, the number of possible permutations is becoming nearly infinite as audiences now traverse social channels with ties to both friends and strangers. Thus, it is more constructive to focus on carefully targeted groups who share not just content but also the experiences and emotions they arouse and to stick with them over the long term.

Every campaign must plug into an audience's experiences. But in a complex social system, those experiences can vary according to the audience, the issues, and the platforms. Channels also provide different perspectives based on their cultures, codes of ethics, and even colloquialisms. Consequently, initiatives must be crafted to leverage the distinct combinations of experiences.

At the same time, social marketers must recognize whether their audiences are multitaskers—flitting from one channel to another—or tend to reside on a single network. If they are the latter, it serves no purpose to shepherd consumers from Facebook to Twitter to Pinterest. In that case, it makes more sense to keep the user experience within the channel it originated and evoke the most powerful emotional response possible.

The Social Ecosystem

Whatever the circumstances, all these elements, either acting independently or continually interacting, make up the social ecosystem, which is the complete set of touch points that propel the creative process. The social ecosystem might be a website or mobile app. Sometimes, it is a social network. At other times, it may be comments and reviews. What matters, though, is how it is activated on behalf of a brand.

That responsibility falls to the content team, whose job it is to develop and implement a robust strategy. The first step is to create a content calendar that accurately reflects a brand's objectives and priorities while simultaneously attracting advocates and promoting audience growth (Figure 17.1). To that end, examining the brand's audience truths can help identify the most appropriate technique for a particular set of experiences.

One such approach is to layer the content so that audience emotions are induced and then reinforced incrementally. Here, lightweight content such as text posts, photo posts, and link promotion regularly sustain

Big Fuel - Content Calendar   BIG❋FUEL
FROM CONTENT TO COMMERCE

Date	Day	Time	Platform	Content	Link	Assets	Char. Count	Status
		10:00	F	"Twitter ads are designed to be human - in a brand's 'voice,' but not robotic - and meld with the content around them." How do you think Twitter's ad platform stacks up against its competitors?	http://www.readwriteweb.com/archives/ads-arent-reshaping-twitter-twitter-is-reshaping-ads.php		193	Published
		10:00	T	Could an ad-free Facebook work? @JoshConstine explores the possibilities. [TECH] (via @TechCrunch)	http://tcrn.ch/QQrrG2		100	Published
10/		10:00	T	**Google+ could be back in the game if it conquers mobile before Facebook does. [LINK] (via @chadcat @TNW)**	**http://tnw.co/Suxvr6**			
		10:00	T	Or, as we like to say, "shareable." (via @parrodickey) RT @peretti 13 Ways To Make Something Go Viral [LINK]	http://bit.ly/SrbfWO		110	Published
		10:00	F	Could Facebook influence age verification around the Web? Facebook recently made recommendations to the FTC regarding The Children's Online Privacy Protection Act. Read the full article on [TAG] InsideFacebook.com. [LINK]	http://bit.ly/UDS95P		221	Published
10/2/12	Tuesday	10:00		Google+ could be back in the game if it conquers mobile before Facebook does. [LINK] (via @chadcat @TNW)	http://tnw.co/Suxvr6		104	Published
		13:00	T	Today's critical reading: Where Facebook Is Looking to Grow, an interview with COO Sheryl Sandberg [LINK] (via @JBoorstin)	http://bit.ly/SXbR02		122	Published
		16:00	T	What's your favorite #SocialTV app? Second Screen Experiences and Why They Work: [LINK] (via @socialmediaclub)	http://bit.ly/UDUbTw		110	Published
		10:00	F	LinkedIn debuted a new blogging platform yesterday that places the professional network square in the middle of the influence game. With its emphasis on quality content and engagement, do you think the follow feature is a good move for LinkedIn? Read the full article on [TAG] Fast Company: [LINK]	http://bit.ly/QAqIis		297	Published
10/3/12	Wednesday	10:00	T	Why Facebook Users Like - and Unlike - brands: [LINK] (via @Janastas @marketingprofs) Which of these stats surprised you?	http://bit.ly/QKGrrX		121	Published
		13:00	T	Mining consumer data just got easier with @EricSchechter's Top 3 Tools for Listening to Social Chatter: [LINK] (@iMediaTweet)	http://bit.ly/Sw950I		125	Published

Figure 17.1   Big Fuel—Content Calendar

and move a conversation forward, whereas less frequent but more compelling content such as video serve as inflection points, often around tent poles. That way, the calendar is constantly populated with relevant content that also adheres to the best practices and production values associated with strong design, interactive technology, and video.

As ideas are being concocted and tossed back and forth, a brand's channel management team is also brought into the process to factor in what is possible across the channels. As Big Fuel's vice president of brand channel management Mandy Gresh explains, one task is to help develop the content calendar:

> In putting together the calendar, we need to know if it encompasses a media website where different content will be posted. Is there a blog? What is being posted on Facebook and Twitter? What are the consistent messages? Then we try to garner news in different ways from different channels. For example, a press release for the media channel doesn't work on Facebook. But maybe one nugget from the release makes great fodder for a Facebook story.

In the Moment

Usually, it is advisable for a brand to adhere fairly closely to the content calendar so that, for example, at the start of every month, it has material firmly in place it can work with. "But there certainly are times when it is necessary to vary from that routine," says Gresh, "because social should be in the moment, and that is critical to determining the value of content, rather than if it is just on the calendar."

Brands that achieve the correct balance between frequency and effect are well positioned to engage with audiences and have their content shared, but the balancing act also requires brand information to be topical and timely. That is where an emotional connection is a crucial asset. Emotions not only help people interpret their world, but do so from moment to moment.[3] So, unless a brand can capture consumers' emotions and hold them over time, it risks losing its audience to another brand with something more compelling to say.

Clearly, then, publishing well-timed content in social media demands a swift review and approval process, and sometimes it requires an approval in preproduction when there might not otherwise be opportunities during production or in postproduction. For example, if a brand is running a live event to support a new product launch, there could be social extensions baked into the execution plan that require the production of real-time, onsite content. The host might be recorded on video for live streaming to off-site locations, or activities throughout the event might be caught on a smartphone camera and immediately posted to the brand's Instagram channel.

Even material not slated for immediate release, such as a recap video, still has a very brief shelf life. Consequently, the production team must turn it around as quickly as possible, including getting consent from marketing management. The general rule of thumb is that the longer it takes to record and release information about an event or incident, the less likely it will be viewed, commented on, or shared. What is more, such rapid response is not limited to videos, photos, or text postings. Design changes to site layouts and social pages often must be done quickly as well. Plus, as networks frequently alter their formats and algorithms, fast learning is also becoming a valuable asset.

That is not to say, however, that all content is time sensitive. As noted previously, there are videos on YouTube and gallery walls on Pinterest that remain popular for months because they are shared, commented on, and added to. What they reveal are universal audience and brand truths that can land on channels anywhere and at any time in a content calendar.

Learning As You Go

In social media marketing, every facet of content production must work like a well-oiled machine, and creative teams must be prepared to produce high-end content in short order. Developments in social video, such as faster end-to-end turnaround time and low-cost systems that come close to matching broadcast equipment, are breaking many of the constraints of conventional TV. The commitment to understanding audiences and delivering what is of real value to them remains intact, however.

Because social media marketing is an octopus that touches so many facets of business, it is wise to build working teams with hybrid players so as to capitalize on their versatile capabilities. Front-end developers with a strong knowledge base of design, designers with a proficiency in user experience, and video producers able to edit their own content working as a team can make a considerable difference in the quality of content on social channels.

Brands must also accept that their creative teams will not always get it just right the first time. A lot of content work in social is trial and error, and brands need to be willing to experiment. Still, there is always something to learn that can be passed on and used more successfully the next time.

Making Connections

Creative content, no matter how well crafted, may be for naught if it remains a well-kept secret. Many marketers, especially those who move from traditional to social media, forget that their work does not end once they have created something. To the contrary, it has only just begun.

Spheres of Influence

Despite the shift in time, attention, and money to owned and earned venues, paid media marketing remains a valuable asset in any marketer's portfolio. It is still one of the most effective ways to launch a new product

Insight

During more than 25 years overseeing traditional and digital media services, Herb Scannell, president of BBC Worldwide Americas, has witnessed dramatic changes, particularly in the area of content distribution.

Programming means thinking about what you are making; thinking about what your audience wants; thinking about how your audience is using it. And then delivering it all on a regular basis. In traditional television, producers deliver tapes and then expect the machine to make magic happen. But in social, the hard work doesn't really begin until after you have "delivered the tape." That is when you have to figure out how you are going to get your audience.

The nature of refining, refining, and refining the way you do on TV with pilots and testing is not something you can or need to do in the social world. Here, you create it, put it up, and then iterate. Or the audience iterates for you, and basically takes control of content and recreates content. And you have to embrace that because the more that your audience is engaged in that way and actually involved with your content, the better off you are. But you have to cultivate that by being real, through real-time conversations. You are not just a cold façade or a corporate entity. You are a relatable brand. And behind the brand are people.

or service, and truly creative spots can generate a considerable amount of buzz, as Super Bowl ads have been proving for decades. Brands also recognize the advantage of spreading their message across multiple media concurrently, however. The "Old Spice man" has become the poster boy for this approach, appearing on the company's website as well as on its YouTube, Facebook, and Twitter channels.

Paid media marketing in the form of advertising has, for generations, influenced people to buy products and services. Or, if Sam Wanamaker is to be believed, only half of all advertising is influential, whereas the other half has just taken up space. Unlike with most traditional marketing, however, social marketers now have to go into overdrive to consider the

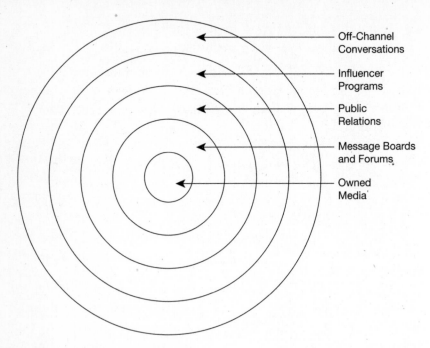

Figure 17.2   Spheres of Influence

many different places where content can be assigned, the various ways consumers might discover it, and the expanding spheres of brand influence (Figure 17.2).

At the core are a brand's owned media. Included here are its website and its presence on channels like Facebook, Twitter, YouTube, Pinterest, and any online property it controls where consumers can congregate to find out information directly about its products and services. Because consumers most likely come to these locations to discuss the brand—either positively or negatively—it is imperative that all messaging be aimed directly, yet tactfully, at introducing the brand into the conversations.

The next sphere of influence includes message boards and forums. Although brands do not control these informal settings, they can use them to their advantage to interact with targeted consumers without having to deal with gatekeepers. Not having control can also be a benefit if a brand can position itself as a conversational peer rather than a powerbroker. Best practices need to be considered, however. For one thing, the brand should have an ongoing presence on these sites. Simply swooping in occasionally to post an ad or pitch a product will accomplish very little except to antagonize participants. Second, whether starting or joining a conversation thread, the brand's contribution has to be topical. Although this point may seem obvious, many companies do not do their homework before engaging consumers.

The third sphere represents one of the oldest forms of influence: public relations. By working closely with their internal public relations team or an outside agency, brands can identify those individuals, organizations, and media that carry weight within their industries. Some may already be organic spokespeople or advocates for a brand. If such people are not immediately accessible, a qualified media relations professional can make the initial connection. The intention is to establish partnerships to create and drive brand-specific messages from their channels to those owned by the brand.

The fourth and probably most important sphere comprises influencer programs. These programs aim at third-party publishers and thought leaders who present some of the best opportunities to contact and effect an audience. The vast majority of the conversations online have little or nothing to do with brands. The challenge, then, is to extend a brand's reach to those places where targeted consumers naturally spend their time, discover relevant conversations, and build relationships with those who create appropriate content.

In this case, *appropriate* means content based on consumers' interests and lifestyles and brand perceptions. Engagement is the stage in the creative process where they intersect. It is also where a brand's objectives are analyzed. Influencers focus on this point when creating content that touches an audience's emotions and addresses a brand's needs.

Moreover, the content must always be expressed through the influencer's voice, not that of the brand. Not only will the message have significantly greater emotional appeal when it comes from the influencer than from the brand, but it is also more apt to be shared. Plus, it gives a brand more credibility. Brands do not define themselves as caring, concerned, or otherwise cool. That is ultimately up to the audience. An influencer can, however, put in a good word or two, especially if and when those words are his own.

The fifth and final sphere of influence includes consumers' off-channel conversations. At this point, brand influence is often the collective outcome of the previous four spheres, and although opportunities here are relatively minimal, they do exist. Here, consumers are targeted with very specific messages around conversations they are having in real time, and they are engaged through one-on-one communications or techniques such as hashtags.

Just as with the convergence of paid, owned, and earned media, successfully working across different spheres is dependent on a great many factors, not the least of which is the consumer. Whatever the circumstances, the goal is to be clear, consistent, and above all, cognizant of what is important to the audience.

Insight

Josh Scheiner, Big Fuel's vice president of content development and distribution, oversees all social campaigns, such as this exciting product launch for Colgate.

Colgate Wisp is a disposable mini-toothbrush that provides a new way of cleaning teeth on the go, and the company knew it was a product worth talking about. Colgate also recognized that its target demographic—active young adults—[was] always online having conversations and seeking interesting content. So it decided to make social media a powerful part of its launch strategy. But since nobody wants to friend or follow a toothbrush, it had to find uniquely engaging ways to talk about Wisp.

From the very beginning, Big Fuel worked with Colgate to test a broad array of concepts to see which ones would stick with consumers. One that definitely stuck out for all of us was the fact that everyone wants to be "kissable." In other words, whether you are going out on a date or going to work or to an interview, you want to be your best and feel self-confident. And the idea of being "kissable" was a terrific ways to represent the brand in social.

To that end, we created an application we called Spin the Wisp, which was a virtual kiss generator. People could populate the wheel with as many as 16 of their friends from their social graph. They would spin the Wisp and it would land on a flavor, a location, and a friend. Then it would send a kiss to that person. It was a great way for Colgate's target audience to flirt with each other.

We also developed a second program called Be the Face of Wisp, *where folks could upload their photo with the product on it and enter a contest where they could invite their friends to vote for them. It turned out to be a highly addictive game with a tremendous amount of response.*

But the part of the campaign that most excited everyone was a video outreach we titled Wisp Underground. *We creatively integrated the Wisp product story into eight different online videos—from how-to to comedy to talk—that tapped into the audiences' interests and passions so that they also became people stories. Then we seeded the videos into every conceivable sharing site online. At the same time, we got the application into the hands of a number of top Facebook influencers and several major bloggers. So not only did we reach consumers across publisher sites, video platforms, influencer networks, and photo applications, but we also gathered a great deal of insight that we could learn from for the future.*

Filling the Gap

Of course, none of this marketing happens in a vacuum. Social networks are parts of larger systems that can exert significant influence on their members. Accordingly, brands also need to consider what is happening in the world—both online and off—that audiences will be sure to talk about. The extent to which a brand does so successfully is reflected in its network tent poles and in the content it creates to further fuel the conversations on either side of those poles.

Every social message must ultimately communicate something about the brand, but it should not do so at the expense of relevance. A brand's priority is to sell its product, whereas its social strategy is to tell its story in such a way that it touches peoples' passions. The value of the network model rests in large part on its capacity to bridge the gap between product stories and the people stories. Effective campaigns find ways to embed this value within the cultural events that make up the tent poles and the meaningful content that surround them.

Keep in Mind . . .

1. Social media campaigns can be thought of as franchises that generate considerable interest among targeted audiences.
2. Most successful campaigns are two-part endeavors. The first part consists of creating compelling content. The second part requires making it as easy as possible for audiences to find it.
3. Every campaign must target specific audiences across multiple platforms and channels, and then it must consistently deliver content that plugs into their interests and emotions.
4. To that end, the content development, content production, and brand channel management teams must work together to create and execute robust and well-timed content strategies.
5. Successful content creation is a learning process involving ongoing trial and error.
6. The process does not end once content is created. Brands must then work across paid, owned, and earned media to ensure that their content reaches the correct audiences.
7. One of the most effective ways to reach the ideal audiences is to leverage various spheres of influence, including influencers, community sites, conventional approaches like public relations, and consumers' off-channel communications.

Notes

1. John Medina, *Brain Rules: 12 Principles for Surviving and Thriving at Work, Home, and School* (Seattle: Pear Press, 2008).
2. David Rock, *Your Brain at Work: Strategies for Overcoming Distraction, Regaining Focus, and Working Smarter All Day Long* (New York: HarperBusiness, 2009).
3. Ibid.

CHAPTER 18

Taking Measure

For the better part of the twentieth century, marketers and their researchers confidently proclaimed: "You can't manage what you don't measure."[1] Today's social media marketers rarely sing that tune, however, and for good reason. Despite adopting an ever-expanding array of social tools and techniques, many brands still do not know what it is they are supposed to measure, nor quite what to expect from the outcomes.

After questioning more than 2,700 social media practitioners in 2012, public relations publisher Lawrence Ragan Communications and the NASDAQ OMX Group found that nearly 70 percent of respondents are either dissatisfied or only "somewhat satisfied" with how they track social media initiatives. Barely 5 percent are "very satisfied."[2] The measurement techniques of those surveyed—from small, medium, and major firms, along with government agencies and nonprofit organizations—are all over the map. Significant majorities monitor web traffic and social interactions such as followers, fans, and likes. Somewhat fewer gauge their brands' reputations, and fewer still keep account of new leads. Only about 30 percent measure sales.

Conversation

What is the return on investment (ROI) of social media?

Matt Tepper, vice president, audience insights, Big Fuel:
    "ROI is a challenge. At this point, there is no common definition
    (continued)

· (*Continued*)

for social. We don't have it and the clients don't have it. So most people still don't know what they're getting for this. It's our job to define ROI. My personal feeling is it has to be customized for each brand."

Nikki Carmel, group director, network development, Big Fuel: "When a brand spends this much money on TV and it hits this many eyeballs, you can measure ROI. But it's hard to do that in social. Right now there is no real number for social ROI and we don't always know where in the funnel to look for it. Sometimes it is awareness. Sometimes it is sales. It depends on what you are trying to do. We are not there yet, but what we can show is engagement, share of voice, and positive sentiment."

Ted Rubin, chief social marketing officer, Collective Bias: "When someone asks me, what is the ROI of social, I ask them, what is the ROI of trust? What is the ROI of loyalty? One of the things I strongly believe is that you can create social credit. I call it social insurance, and to me it is the most valuable return on investment you can get from social. If you are always open and authentic and others see that in you, that's what I call social insurance. And by building those kinds of relationships, when you need the help of others—whether it is during a crisis or you are running a campaign to raise money for a good cause, people will be there."

Three Decision Pillars

Accurate measurement standards have become moving targets as they are increasingly linked to cultural shifts, evolving brand needs, and changing social strategies. Moreover, the growing number of channels and platforms across which social activities occur—and the convergence of paid, owned, and earned media—propels an ongoing confluence of methods. In addition, brands will continue to seek the holy grail of measurement, that perfect correlation between online encounters and sales, both online and offline.

Where do social marketers begin? "Start at the end, and trace your way back to the beginning," says Matt Tepper, Big Fuel's vice president of audience insights. What sounds like the sort of advice Alice may have received in Wonderland is actually the basis for measuring outcomes in the network model. "Measurement should always be done backwards," says Tepper. "We have to be able to know what decisions need to be made before we can determine what analysis can inform those decisions, and before we can land on what data is required to do that analysis."

Within the network model are three fundamental pillars on which all critical decisions essentially rest:

1. **Inspiration:** Ensuring that content is relevant and meaningful
2. **Distribution:** Understanding how best to publish content
3. **Scorekeeping:** Quantifying success to determine whether to expand, maintain, or decrease individual program or tactics

Productively measuring each of these pillars can be a considerable problem, however, because social media networks, like all things digital, generate vast amounts of data. Indeed, there is more raw data to cull from than ever before, and even information that has been fully vetted and analyzed does not always produce valuable insights. It is little wonder that a majority of global marketing practitioners believe that they face a "significant challenge" in their ability to measure marketing effectiveness.[3]

Moreover, so much of that input now arrives at accelerating speeds, even though such immediacy is not always compulsory. Real-time information, as part of the network model, supports tactical channel management decisions, but the same set of pillars can also be used to inform more strategic recommendations. These proposals appear in regularly scheduled reports that can be delivered monthly, quarterly, or even twice a year based on a brand's objectives (Figure 18.1). Clear lines must therefore be drawn between what information is needed day to day and what can be provided less frequently.

Inspiration

To furnish the most relevant content, community managers need to know, in real time, everything that is happening within their social neighborhoods, including the key topics and trends that will enable them to efficiently administer their brand's network. A great deal of this information comes from social listening tools such as Crimson Hexagon, Netbase, and Brandwatch, which can pinpoint timely material related to the brand's

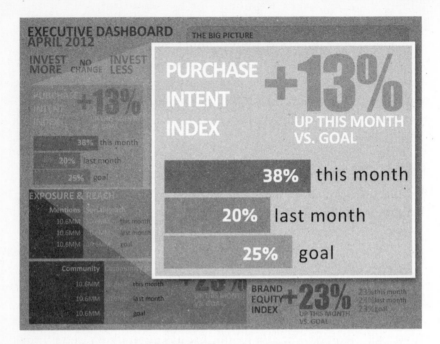

Figure 18.1   Sample of Scheduled Reporting Dashboard Excerpt

audience, its industry, and the brand itself. Inspirational content also comes from sources like Facebook posts, Twitter feeds, and conventional news media, all of which are categorized, prioritized, and visualized.

Less frequent is the need to analyze content patterns. Because successful brand-consumer relationships take time to build, with the goal of lasting long term, it is crucial to accurately track the style, tone, and quality of content over an extended period.

Unfortunately, no technology currently exists to support deep content analysis. Consequently, every post, every tweet, every piece of distributed content must be categorized by hand. Still, it is possible to analyze patterns in content—without skewing the data as a result of one or two posts that perform exceptionally well or poorly—and provide recommendations as to what content works best in different circumstances.

Distribution

Just about every brand's goal is to be repeatedly mentioned in social media throughout the day, as positively as possible, and community

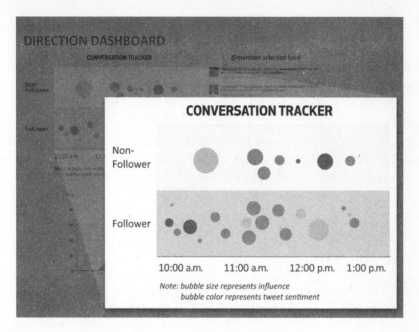

Figure 18.2   Sample of Real-Time Dashboard Excerpt

managers must participate in as many of those conversations as possible. Despite these lofty goals, however, most distribution decisions cannot, and should not, be made based on daily data. In fact, there are only two such decisions that real-time data can support: outreach prioritization and paid media recommendations (Figure 18.2).

By using social listening tools (such as Crimson Hexagon, Netbase, and Brandwatch) in combination with influencer identification tools (such as SocMetrics), community managers can prioritize decisions with the goal of maximizing the effect of conversations they choose to participate in. Most often, it means arranging mentions determined by how influential a particular person is as well as the sentiment that person expresses. Highly recognized influencers and advocates always receive the most attention. Negative mentions should be addressed first, followed by positive mentions and, finally, neutral mentions.

Real-time tweet and post performance data are critical for supporting paid media applications. This information, achieved by analyzing content decay, provides recommendations for what types of content should be amplified by paid dollars. Without paid media support, almost all content decomposes very quickly in the social sphere, often within the first two hours. For some forms of content, however, the destruction happens less rapidly. That content is more likely to spread widely and is best amplified with paid media.

From a more strategic perspective, scheduled distribution reports provide recommendations to improve the overall social ecosystem. In part, they do so by clarifying what content needs to be distributed within each channel, by time of day or day of the week. Reports also include audience profiles to help gauge if there have been any significant shifts among audiences within channels or with respect to a brand's social presence.

Scorekeeping

As is the case with both inspiration and distribution, daily scorekeeping is very different than keeping score on a less frequent basis. Although it is not necessary to track success or failure of social marketing from one day to the next, scorekeeping is vital to distinguishing large spikes or dips in key performance indicators so as to draw attention to possible crises.

In the longer term, scorekeeping is used to perform trend analysis around key performance indicators to measure if campaigns or other social initiatives are succeeding or failing against the predetermined goals. Often, this analysis examines a combination of social media data along with other data sets, such as web analytics or sales data.

A Work in Progress

Every brand wants to measure, as timely and as accurately as it can, its social marketing tactics and strategies. As social media opportunities grow and the marketing mix evolves, the process becomes even more complex.

Outcomes are hard to measure in complex systems because cause and effect are not always closely related in time or space. Some answers may be obvious immediately. It may take a while before other consequences are identified, however, and sometimes that may not occur until after first reaching several false conclusions. Successful social marketing is, after all, a process of trial and error.

Still, some results can be planned for, so they can also be measured, and even though there is no single "best" metric, there are a variety of methods to gauge how content contributes to conversations. A great many other results, however, are unexpected. They cannot be readily measured, at least not by conventional means. They can and should be analyzed and evaluated, however, because they may provide far better insights than any standard metric.

Imperative, too, is the realization that complexity is nonlinear. As much as brands prefer to present ideas in logical sequence, complex systems subsist in the form of feedback loops. Every decision or action produces new information that may either substantiate or undermine our original assumptions. Therefore, because every effect can loop back and possibly alter strategies, it is difficult to definitively measure outcomes.

Keep in Mind . . .

1. Most brand marketers are still unsure about what it is they should be measuring in social media.
2. Effective social metrics identify not only the correct information to be measured, but also the appropriate time to do so.
3. In the network model, there are three key pillars that underlie all types of decisions: inspiration, which ensures that content is relevant; distribution, which establishes the best means to publish content; and scorekeeping, which determines if, when, and how to modify campaigns or tactics.

Notes

1. The phrase has been incorrectly attributed to American management consultant W. Edwards Deming, who actually believed that one of the "seven deadly diseases of management" was running a company solely on visible figures.
2. Russell Working, "Most Unhappy with Social Media Measurement, Survey Says," *Ragan.com*, December 10, 2012, www.ragan.com/Main/Articles/5bcbd896-a7ce -4335-85c5-875597524c67.aspx.
3. IBM, "The State of Marketing: 2012 IBM's Global Survey of Marketers," *SlideShare*, June 5, 2012, www.slideshare.net/165yohodr/the-state-of-marketing-2012-ibms -global-survey-of-marketers-final.

SECTION V

Looking Ahead

CHAPTER 19

Looking Out

There is a favorite practice among digital pundits: when they want to describe the vast reach of social media, they will compare social networks to nations. You have probably heard it said that if Facebook were a country, it would be the third largest in the world. For their parts, Twitter would be fourth and Google+ would come in at fifth place. In fact, six channels would rank among the world's most populous nations (Figure 19.1). Such comparisons not only underscore social media's popularity, but can also help a brand succeed in the expanding social ecosystem.

Imagine doing business for the first time in a different country, say one of the so-called emerging markets. As a group, these countries are some of the fastest growing economies in the world. Their aggregate populations account for about one-third of all consumer spending worldwide, and they have regularly outspent their American counterparts for the past five years. What is more, emerging market economies are extremely diverse, from behemoth China to up-and-coming Bangladesh.

Although still relatively new to the global economic stage, each of these countries already has an established set of social and cultural norms, customs, currencies, laws, regulations, and infrastructures that influence their marketing practices. They are not new—in fact, they existed long before you arrived—but they are new to you, and you will have to adjust the way you do business if you hope to succeed there.

Emerging Social Markets

Now think of social media in the same way. Contrary to conventional wisdom, social media outlets have been around for quite a while. In

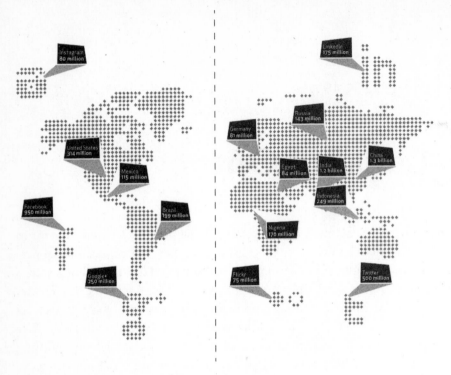

Figure 19.1 Social Channel Reach and Scale

digital form, they are as old as the Internet itself, going back more than 40 years. One of the principal objectives in creating the first computer network system was to enable engineers and computer scientists in various parts of the country to communicate directly with one another without having to go through a central gatekeeper. The technical term is a rhizomatic network, which simply means that any node (a person, text, image, or sound) on the network can connect with any other node, regardless of how big or complicated the network becomes.

Initially, just a handful of individuals at four universities—Stanford; University of California, Los Angeles; University of California, Santa Barbara; and University of Utah—connected across what was then known as the ARPANET.[1] As additional networks were folded in, they brought with them thousands, and then millions of new users who shared information across bulletin boards, listservs, multiuser domains, Usenet groups, and professional services such as CompuServe and America Online. By the beginning of the twenty-first century, AOL was the Internet's 800-pound gorilla, with more than 30 million paid subscribers who regularly participated in its chat rooms, virtual communities, and instant messaging. Not long after came Friendster, MySpace, and then Facebook.

As with emerging market nations, social networks are among the fastest growing parts of the Internet, attracting more than a billion regular users and accounting for an increasing amount of hours and dollars spent online. They are also an equally assorted lot. At one end of the spectrum is colossal Facebook. At the other are the niche channel Path, a personal social network for close friends and family, and the even smaller and more intimate Pair, which connects just two people.

In addition, social media networks have developed their own set of customs, conducts, standards, and rules. Some are particular to individual channels, like LinkedIn's professional, business-oriented culture or Twitter's 140-character limit. Others, however, are norms that transcend almost all networks, such as that two-way conversation has replaced one-way communication; control has gradually shifted from brands to consumers; and routine advertising, which is interruptive on conventional media, can become intrusive on social media outlets.

Mutual Relationships

Newly arrived nations and networks have also disrupted the dynamics of multinational organizations. In many parts of the world, large, established firms must now compete for consumers' time, attention, and wallets with smaller and more nimble local competitors who are often more attuned to their respective markets. The same is true on various networks where start-up firms and individual upstarts are more at home in the social environment. In both cases, many companies must hire people with new knowledge and skills while also training existing employees how to adapt.

Perhaps the most compelling connection between emerging nations and social networks is that development of the former will surely affect growth of the latter. More than half of all Facebook users, for example, live beyond the borders of Europe and North America. What is more, interest in social networking is growing in low- and middle-income countries such as Brazil, Egypt, India, Mexico, and Turkey, while engagement is waning in some of the richest nations, such as Germany and Japan.[2]

Insight

As the founder and former chief executive officer of Vitrue, which helps clients amplify their social messages, Reggie Bradford has worked with some of the world's leading media companies and consumer brands.

Historically, there have been "tent-pole" events that are truly global in nature, like the Olympics, the World Cup, and the Super Bowl. And they were once the only mechanisms to be able to communicate and reach a global audience. But with social, that game has changed. Brands now have the opportunity to create and message with a global audience on a daily and even hourly basis. So by creating a global infrastructure, with a consistent look and feel, consistent navigation, and a consistent user experience, it is more practical than ever to maintain a global brand integrity.

As in the United States—where users of social media are overwhelmingly urban, more affluent, and better educated than in other parts of the world—participation elsewhere is also more widespread and growing faster inside metropolitan areas, where nearly 70 percent of residents are active users.[3] In emerging markets, both the number and size of market cities are expanding dramatically, so much so that within the next dozen years, as many as 440 such urban centers will add nearly 2 billion more members to the planet's consumer class and will contribute almost half of the growth to their countries' gross domestic products.[4]

Going Mobile

Moreover, given that most of their telecommunications infrastructure is built around mobile technologies rather than fixed, emerging market consumers will help drive the ultimate dominance of mobile social media. Since the start of the twenty-first century, the number of portable devices in emerging nations has increased 1,700 percent and exceeds those in developed countries by about three to one.[5] In fact, data from

Cisco suggest that there may be more mobile-connected devices on the globe than there are people to use them.[6]

As a result, the fastest growth among all social networks will take place in the Middle East, Africa, and Asia Pacific, all of which already post higher than average growth rates (Figure 19.2).[7] In parts of Asia Pacific, social networks also exert more influence over consumers when they are making brand decisions.[8] Their effect is likely to become even more powerful as people become more and more accustomed to using mobile devices throughout the day. Indeed, research from Google shows that 65 percent of shoppers start the online purchase process on their smartphones.[9]

Doing Social Business around the World

Poke a wet finger in the air and you cannot help notice that economic winds are blowing east to new markets outside the United States, Europe, and Japan; brands of all kinds will have to follow suit to engage with billions of new consumers worldwide. These same consumers, along with hundreds of millions of their counterparts in the more developed nations, will also pull companies into the social sphere as they spend increasing amounts of their waking hours online.

Thus, brands doing business in both emerging markets and social media will have to learn a different set of ground rules. The key will be recognizing the significant economic, social, cultural, and political differences within regions and between countries. Taking those factors into account makes them both more manageable.

Once brands have made those distinctions, they need people on the ground who understand the platforms that make up the whole social environment in various regions (and they are not always Facebook or Twitter) and grasp the distribution network and the cultural nuances that come out of those parts of the world. Then, management can start to develop an end-to-end strategy. Now, however, it is still a question of what market stage a nation or region is in. Although differences will always prevail among geographic areas, by employing a comprehensive network model and applying universal business solutions, it will be possible to standardize many social marketing practices over the long term, both globally and locally.

	2010	2011	2012	2013	2014
Middle East & Africa	**38.5%**	**33.8%**	**31.8%**	**23.6%**	**15.8%**
Asia Pacific	**30.7%**	**27.5%**	**24.8%**	**21.1%**	**14.5%**
—India	38.8%	51.5%	51.7%	37.9%	23.2%
—Indonesia	54.8%	51.4%	51.6%	23.8%	18.0%
—China*	33.2%	23.9%	19.9%	19.1%	13.2%
—Japan	17.1%	20.7%	13.1%	7.0%	6.0%
—Australia	16.3%	17.1%	11.7%	9.8%	8.4%
—South Korea	8.2%	13.2%	9.9%	8.1%	5.2%
—Other	43.4%	46.1%	28.8%	25.7%	19.1%
Latin America	**27.2%**	**20.8%**	**18.5%**	**14.6%**	**11.5%**
—Mexico	35.0%	18.4%	27.9%	16.2%	13.8%
—Brazil	16.5%	19.0%	13.5%	13.1%	9.7%
—Argentina	39.4%	22.0%	12.7%	11.5%	9.9%
—Other	33.9%	23.4%	21.1%	16.0%	12.6%
Eastern Europe	**22.2%**	**14.9%**	**12.0%**	**12.6%**	**9.5%**
—Russia	19.4%	11.6%	11.3%	11.2%	8.1%
—Other	23.9%	16.9%	12.4%	13.3%	10.2%
Western Europe	**27.2%**	**18.0%**	**11.9%**	**9.7%**	**7.1%**
—Germany	26.7%	20.8%	13.7%	11.1%	7.0%
—Italy	47.6%	27.8%	13.0%	10.3%	8.0%
—Spain	33.5%	18.8%	13.0%	11.5%	8.8%
—France	23.5%	12.2%	10.1%	7.6%	5.8%
—UK	15.0%	9.9%	8.1%	7.0%	6.0%
—Other	30.7%	21.9%	13.5%	10.9%	7.4%
North America	**18.3%**	**9.5%**	**6.6%**	**4.1%**	**4.0%**
—United States	19.1%	9.8%	6.8%	4.1%	4.0%
—Canada	11.2%	6.8%	4.7%	4.6%	4.4%
Worldwide	27.3%	21.8%	19.3%	16.3%	11.9%

Figure 19.2 Social Network User Growth Worldwide, by Region and Country, 2010–2014 (% change)

*excludes Hong Kong.

Note: Internet users who use a social network site via any device at least once per month.

Source: eMarketer, August 2012.

Conversation

How will the continuing growth of mobile affect social media?

- **Reggie Bradford, senior vice president of product development, Oracle:** "We are seeing mobile becoming the first screen for consumers. [At Oracle,] we have research which shows that 50 percent of Facebook usage and Twitter usage is on a mobile device; and social networking is the second most frequented activity on mobile devices. Yet many marketers don't optimize their apps for a mobile experience. So if you are not thinking mobile first, you are potentially missing 50 percent of the audience."
- **Jason Hirschhorn, owner, ReDEF Group:** "I think engagement goes up with mobile, ultimately because you can access from anywhere. You don't have to sit down at a computer. Mobile means that everyone becomes social at some point because it is a remote control to your life. It is everything in your hand."
- **Rikard Steiber, global marketing director, mobile and social advertising, Google:** "People who are heavily vested in traditional media have had a hard time embracing digital media. We are seeing the same thing now with mobile. But people who grew up with mobile are embracing it. Mobile will probably be the main way we access the Internet. It's going to be such a natural part of it. And when we are on our mobile devices we are probably even more social, and in more of a sharing mode."
- **Stephanie Agresta, senior vice president, global director of social media and digital, MSLGROUP** "I think more and more brands are going to program for mobile from the start and not look at mobile as an afterthought. Mobile has got to be where you start thinking about the consumer experience, and not first build a website and then back into the mobile experience."

Insight

Josh Scheiner is a creative marketing executive specializing in social media and promotions-based marketing initiatives.

Companies have to be very conscientious of what social media means in different parts of the world. For example, in Japan, blogging is more complex than simply using something like Facebook, because there is a greater concern over personal privacy. Conversation looks very different there. But there are still subjects around which the culture comes together to discuss; and there are certain subsets of that culture that share their passions. In Japan, their versions of social media are bigger than Facebook is here. Social media is also a phenomenon you see in China and Russia. The mechanics of it may be dramatically different; and the topics of conversations are also different. Yet it's still a digital medium in which people converse. And it provides a great opportunity for brands to participate.

In the meantime, brands can start by rethinking strategies that are based on methods that were first established in older economies and media. Although neither these nations nor networks are new, they do present new challenges and opportunities for brands approaching either for the first time.

Keep in Mind . . .

1. Social media and emerging market economies have both been around for quite a while, even though they may be unfamiliar to new entrants.
2. Just as they will have to compete with smaller, more nimble competitors in new markets, companies may also be outmaneuvered on social media by more savvy newcomers.
3. Interest in social media is much faster in low- and middle-income countries like Brazil and India than in wealthier nations such as Germany and Japan.
4. The growth of mobile social media is being driven in large part by developed countries, where social networking exerts significant influence over consumers' brand decisions.

Notes

1. The ARPANET was the world's first operational packet switching computer network. Multiple other independent networks connected with it, ultimately evolving into today's global Internet.

2. Pew Research Center, "Social Networking Popular across Globe," *Pew Global Attitudes Project*, December 12, 2012, www.pewglobal.org/2012/12/12/social-networking-popular-across-globe/.

3. Sara, "The Average Social Media User, Part 1," *Lab42*, February 21, 2012, http://blog.lab42.com/the-average-social-media-user-part-1.

4. Richard Dobbs, Jaana Remes, and Fabian Schaer, "Unlocking the Potential of Emerging-Market Cities," *McKinsey Quarterly*, September 2012, https://www.mckinseyquarterly.com/Unlocking_the_potential_of_emerging-market_cities_3015.

5. David Yanofsky and Christopher Mims, "Since 2000, the Number of Mobile Phones in the Developing world Has Increased 1700%," Quartz, October 2012, http://qz.com/9101/mobile-phones-developing-world/.

6. "There Will Be More Smartphones Than Humans by Year's End," *Mashable*, February 14, 2012, http://mashable.com/2012/02/14/more-smartphones-than-humans/.

7. "Emerging Markets Lead World in Social Networking Growth," *eMarketer*, August 16, 2012, www.emarketer.com/PressRelease.aspx?R=1009275.

8. "Consumers in Asia-Pacific More Responsive to Social Endorsements," *eMarketer*, July 16, 2012, www.public.site2.mirror2.phi.emarketer.com/Article.aspx?R=1009190.

9. Laurie Sullivan, "Multiscreen Ad Targeting Connects with Consumer Experience," *Online Media Daily*, August 29, 2012, www.mediapost.com/publications/article/181829/multiscreen-ad-targeting-connects-with-consumer-ex.html?edition=50597#axzz2EHRKAWyr.

CHAPTER 20

Looking In

Social media's increasingly predominant role in brand marketing is becoming a given. If there is a debate any more, it has shifted from "If?" or "When?" to "How?" and there is no shortage of available answers to the question. Too many of the supposed solutions, however, still focus on the separate pieces of the complex puzzle that is social media marketing.

Instead, brands need to recognize that social media marketing is an essential part of everything they do in every stage of the process, whether it is driving awareness, building the brand, acquiring customers, increasing sales, or providing customer support. All stages are geared to establishing loyal and long-term relationships with consumers. "Social cuts across a lot of different things without some people even knowing it," says Andy Markowitz, GE's director of global digital strategy. "Listening for intelligence. Listening for leads. Listening for competitive information. Listening for the comments and complaints that you know are red flags. Those in my world are all part of social."

Toward the Social Organization

As marketing professionals increase their knowledge of social networks and networking, they will likely find themselves sharing their experience and skills across even more touch points, not only outside their organizations, but also within their own four walls. Indeed, companies that have previously made improving relationships with consumers and other external stakeholders their top social media priority are now beginning to turn their attention inward and are applying many of the same techniques across the enterprise.

Nearly every large—and many smaller—organizations are still hierarchical, so a good deal of their knowledge remains imprisoned within silos. Although information confined to individual departments or operations may be easier to coordinate and therefore more cost effective, real innovation seldom occurs within silos. Rather, it emerges at points where separate ideas intersect. That is why companies are starting to use social networks to improve collaboration and significantly reduce the time and effort required to locate critical ideas and information.

McKinsey and Company estimates that such efforts could raise corporate productivity levels by as much as 20 to 25 percent by weaning workers off of conventional one-to-one communications like e-mail and phone calls, and moving them to social channels that facilitate the many-to-many types of connections.[1] The average "interaction worker," notes McKinsey, spends close to 30 percent of the workweek handling e-mail and nearly 20 percent either looking for information or locating colleagues to help carry out specific tasks. Social tools that enable organizations to convert all forms of messages into searchable content can cut the time it takes employees to find company information by up to 35 percent.

As is often the case, however, there are caveats, and McKinsey acknowledges that, so far, few companies have taken full advantage of these technologies, which have generated "only a small fraction of the potential value they can create."[2] That has not stopped champions of social organizations from heralding their merit. Gartner has gone so far as to suggest the emergence of a new form of capitalism forged by the Facebook generation, "in which the values and behaviors that pervade the Internet will also be adopted by innovative and disruptive businesses."[3] Moreover, exhorts Gartner's research vice president Nigel Raynor, "With half the world's population under the age of 25, this may happen sooner than many think."

Perhaps that is true, yet when social marketing software firm DachisGroup polled business leaders from 56 large U.S. and European companies already engaged in social initiatives, more than half admitted that only about 10 to 20 percent of their employees are actively involved in social collaboration.[4] It may be that capturing and capitalizing on ideas can be difficult for organizations. According to a report from the New York American Marketing Association and Columbia Business School's

Center on Global Brand Leadership, the number-one obstacle to taking advantage of such opportunities is the lack of sharing between departments.[5]

To be sure, internal barriers to communication have long been a complication for most organizations, and the introduction of social media will likely add to the complexity. For every company that has embraced social media, many more fail to see the benefits and have continued to stay away. Some changes are surely inevitable, however, and marketing professionals, especially those with social media experience, can play a key role in bringing them about.

Conversation

As companies begin to shift their focus to fostering internal social collaboration and dialogue, what can they do to ensure success?

Ted Rubin, chief social marketing officer, Collective Bias: "Social needs to be a shell around everything you do. I call it social, not social media, because social media is a subset of social. People have to stop thinking of it as separate things and think of it as part of a whole. But it is very complex."

Andy Markowitz, director, global digital strategy, GE: "You have to standardize social skills development. There needs to be social training so that social is a part of everybody's job, because it is the only way to create scalability. I'm not talking about homogenizing and dumbing it down. I'm talking about making it scalable in ways that you can implement."

Reggie Bradford, senior vice president of product development, Oracle: "Another consideration is the CIO [chief information officer] function, which in some respects has been on the sidelines regarding social because marketers have really driven the technology implementation. But if you think about the CIO as a partner to the CMO [chief marketing officer], they have a treasure trove of data that they have been building in the enterprise for years, and the challenge that social has had is, how do you marry the enterprise data you have with the social data you are collecting?"

Stephanie Agresta, global director of social media and digital, MSLGROUP: "I really believe that ultimately it is the culture of an organization that does or does not foster that kind of work. If you look at organizations that have done social in very integrated ways, they probably are more collaborative culturally. I also believe buy-in has to come from above. You can only get so far without leadership committing to supporting these game changes in a structured way."

Keep in Mind . . .

1. Beyond marketing, the use of social media increasingly cuts across all facets of an enterprise.
2. Organizations that effectively implement internal social communication and collaboration initiatives can improve productivity by upward of 25 percent.
3. So far, however, only a handful of large companies have been able to successfully deploy such technologies and systems.

Notes

1. McKinsey Global Institute, "The Social Economy: Unlocking Value and Productivity Through Social Technologies," McKinsey and Company, July 2012, www.mckinsey.com/insights/mgi/research/technology_and_innovation/the_social_economy.
2. Jacques Bughin, Michael Chui, and James Manyika, "Capturing Business Value with Social Technologies," *McKinsey Quarterly*, November 2012, https://www.mckinsey quarterly.com/Strategy/Growth/Capturing_business_value_with_social_technologies_3029.
3. "Gartner Says Capitalism Going Social Will Require Organizations to Build Two-Way Relationships with the '99 Percent,'" *Gartner*, December 3, 2012, www .gartner.com/it/page.jsp?id=2260917.
4. Robert Berkman, "They Built It, but Employees Aren't Coming," *MIT Sloan Management Review*, October 23, 2012, http://sloanreview.mit.edu/improvisations/

2012/10/23/they-built-it-but-employees-arent-coming/?utm_source=feedburner&
utm_medium=feed&utm_campaign=Feed%3A+mitsmr+%28MIT+Sloan+
Management+Review%29&utm_content=Google+Reader#.UNTWlnf8mSq.

5. "Marketers Struggle to Link Digital Data to 'Big Data' Picture," *eMarketer*, March 19,
2012, www.emarketer.com/Article.aspx?id=1008909&R=1008909.

SECTION VI

Epilogue

CHAPTER 21

The Question

At a time when change is just about the only constant, marketers are faced with the formidable challenge of keeping pace with new and still emerging social systems and technologies. In the midst of this seemingly endless progression of conversion and complexity, there is occasionally the urge to pull back, reflect, and wonder how you might do it differently if you had the opportunity to do it all over again.

Thirteen prominent social media thought leaders and practitioners—my fellow Social Media Advertising Consortium board members—were asked to do just that when I posed the following question:

> As professionals and thought leaders in the social space, part of our everyday job seems to be helping organizations understand and embrace the tenants of social media. To a lot of people, it is a "weapon of mass destruction"—it wreaks havoc—as they simply do not understand it, are unclear how to leverage it, and are unable to understand how it has fundamentally changed the marketing and communications landscape forever. Many organizations still suffer from legacy issues and lack the maturity that can make them more "social by design." So . . .

If you were going to build a marketing organization from scratch today, how would you do it?

Scott Monty
Global Digital and Multimedia Communications Manager, Ford

Scott Monty

Over the past two decades, the rise of the Internet has given marketers better tools to be able to plan and measure their work. From site analytics to performance data, open rates, cookie tracking, and online profiles, we probably know more about consumers than ever before. And although the term *marketing science* has only been in existence for 50 years, the practice is poised to achieve a new significance with the ability to capture data via multiple social networks.

When analysts are predicting that the CMO [chief marketing officer] will outspend the CIO [chief information officer] on technology within five years, it's time to ask ourselves how this newfound commitment to technology will play out. How will marketers use predictive and behavioral analytics to inform future campaigns? More importantly, how will this frontline information be effectively relayed to product development teams in addition to the traditional market research that's being done? Ultimately, how will it all weave together to drive growth? These are important questions to ponder and unravel as we look to harness big data.

But, as we know, marketing is not simply a quantitative practice. The reams of additional data are encouraging (if we can figure out how to make sense of it all), but a numbers-driven approach is hardly a formula for success. Volume without sentiment is meaningless.

As much as we might be able to discern user likes and habits from Facebook, Google, and others, even these social data are not enough to differentiate the marketing organization of the future. If we are to embrace how marketing will look and function, we need to stop thinking like marketers and begin to think more like consumers.

One of the great promises of social media is that it transcends traditional channels like advertising and direct marketing, in that it allows us to hypertarget and have a two-way dialog. And yet, for the most part, we've treated it like a new mass marketing channel as we try to build likes, followers, and subscribers. We develop the most sophisticated and clever campaigns and we applaud ourselves for our creative efforts—but have we stopped to consider how the average consumer thinks about this?

Capturing attention is notoriously difficult, and certainly the high-quality executions attract more notice; but one has to wonder, is that enough? Driving up in a flashy car or sporting the most fashionable clothes will get you attention, but we can't run the risk of being the bore at a party who shows up, hands out his business card to everyone, and then leaves. Consumers expect more from us. They expect to be heard and for brands to do something with what they've heard.

It seems as though it's part of the price of doing business, but you would think that the brand managers, marketers, and communicators who are looking to reach new audiences via different platforms would actually take the time to familiarize themselves with communities by being full-fledged members. Only then can we more fundamentally understand what consumers expect from brands in such settings and then go design programs that reflect that—not to mention that we then have the ability to be first responders and trusted members of the communities in which we're trying to do business.

Marketing technology will be a huge opportunity as we move forward, and not only will data help to measure our marketing successes, but it will also help to define future efforts and even products coming out of marketing organizations of the future. Add to that the need for a more human and empathetic approach based in basic psychology and sociology, and we'll see a much more well-rounded marketing organization that fundamentally understands its mission rather than one that waits for quarterly research to indifferently tell it what to do.

Ranked by Forbes *magazine as one of the Top 10 Influencers in Social Media, Scott Monty has been recognized as "a visionary" by the CEO of Ford Motor Company, Alan Mulally.*

As global digital and multimedia communications manager, Monty is a strategic advisor on all social media activities across the company—from blogger relations to marketing support, customer service, and internal communications—as the use of social media is integrated into many facets of Ford business. He has been featured in hundreds of news and business publications in print and on the web, in dozens of books, and on a variety of mainstream media, including NBC, NPR, CNN, *and the* Wall Street Journal. *He is a recognized thought leader in the social media industry and frequently speaks at industry events. In addition to his professional responsibilities, Monty is an active blogger and podcaster, and he is credited with coining the* Oxford Dictionary of English–*accepted term "tweetup."*

B. Bonin Bough
Vice President of Global Media and Consumer Engagement, Mondeléz International

B. Bonin Bough

My perspective on what makes a great marketing organization is really a result of the way my career has evolved over the past 15 or so years. I cut my teeth in marketing through digital and social media, first on the agency side, then in-house at PepsiCo, before arriving at Mondeléz International (formerly Kraft Foods) in early 2012 to fill a much broader role as VP of global media and consumer engagement, with responsibility for all forms of media globally, including leading and developing the partnerships, internal capabilities, and strategies across all forms of consumer connections, including digital, TV, print, and outdoors. Through these different lenses, I've seen firsthand that social media, along with the meteoric rise of mobile and big data, has been an explosive force. It's changed the way we create, disperse, and consume content, and because of that, it has fundamentally changed the way we work as marketers. With more channels to push out content to than ever before, in addition to the traditional channels like TV and print, many marketing organizations have made progress on social, but haven't found the right solution to make their organizations experts about integrated media, across the board.

So, if I were going to build a marketing organization from scratch today, I'd aim not only to make it social by design, but also more integrated by design, by focusing on three big ideas.

1. Social Listening

There are certainly basic guidelines that social media experts adhere to, but often what's working and what's not working can change at the drop of a hat. Because of that, social listening is becoming critical to understanding the inner workings of consumers: the access to real-time data on everyone from the everyday impulse shopper to the savvy price-comparing consumer is unprecedented, and I think many marketers are still not tapping into the full potential of the wealth of information out there. In beginning a new marketing organization, I'd look to hire marketers who aren't satisfied with current measurement tools, who want to innovate social listening to be faster, more nuanced, and even beyond that, natural teachers who are always looking to share learnings across the organization. It's a hiring strategy not foreign to newer online media, like BuzzFeed and Mashable; these publications were built on a bevy of talent and knowledge in social listening from the start, and have thrived accordingly.

2. Acting like a Media Organization

The best media organizations today have mastered how to create content for all audiences across all mediums, fueled by the urgency to stay relevant. Successful publications (and the editors/executives who run them) are some of the most nimble and talented content creators, and they are constantly reinventing themselves, whether you look at the rise of digital subscription models or the way they've mastered breaking news via Twitter. Also, as natural storytellers, these publications are not bent on pushing a message, but crafting a narrative that readers can participate in, and marketers should be, and for the most part are, moving toward this credo, but they need to move faster.

Early on, I'd look to the editors who have been in the trenches of these publications over the past few years and heed their advice in building the organization from the ground up. By the nature of their craft, many of the individuals in media are experts across different media—like TV, online video, web, and social—as often they're not as segmented as marketing organizations, bringing me to my next point.

3. Leaving Mediums Out of Titles

Lastly, and perhaps most crucially, I'd leave "social media" and other media out of titles—whether those were titles of individuals, divisions, or departments. Everyone would be well-rounded media practitioners and have a solid basis of knowledge in media like social—or, would be on the road to getting there and *expected* to get there. No one person or team would be named the "social" or "digital" strategy go-to, and therefore, no one person or team would be *in charge* of social or digital or any other type of strategy. While this may sound like semantics, it often doesn't play out that way, especially in large organizations. Distributing responsibilities makes everyone accountable, which fundamentally changes culture from a focus on mastery to a focus on curiosity and constant learning. If we've learned anything from the rise of new media as marketers, it's that maintaining unfaltering curiosity is just as important as honing other, more traditional marketing skills.

By starting fresh, without divisions or individuals titled by medium, the organization would be able to move more toward an integrated approach where everyone was expected and empowered to have a voice across media, work more like a media organization, and keep their eyes and ears on consumer conversations.

In his current role at Mondeléz International, B. Bonin Bough is responsible for all forms of media, including leading and developing the partnerships, internal capabilities, and strategies across all forms of consumer connections (digital, TV, print, and outdoors). He was recognized as one of business' hottest rising stars in Fortune's 2011 "40 Under 40" list as well as Fast Company's "2011 100 Most Creative People in Business" and Ebony's *"Power 100" list. Bough's achievements in the world of interactive marketing have won him numerous awards, including a Webby, Stevie, Golden Pencil, Sabre, Big Apple, Com Arts, and SXSW Viewer's Choice. He is coauthor of the 2010 book* Perspectives on Social Media Marketing, *cochair of the Digital Collective, and a member of the board of the Social Media Advisory Council.*

Leslie Reiser
Director of WW Digital Marketing,
IBM General Business

Leslie Reiser

Like anything that is seen as "breaking tradition," social media has not been widely understood and even less effectively leveraged. Enthusiastically adopted by the more savvy individuals in its early years, developed into profitable new business models by some, it is surprising that many brands and seasoned marketers still don't get it. Thousands of examples exist on how social media can be a powerful extension of your brand—a way to amplify your voice, extend your message, develop advocacy, and uncover opportunity. Yet there are a small number of cases where the social web has been hijacked for nefarious purposes, either deliberately or inadvertently. It is from those instances that the uncertainty has grown.

Since these instances are relatively few, the modern-day enterprise needs to address its paranoia. While social media can certainly be used to inflict pain (deliberate) or have unintended consequences (inadvertent), the vast majority of organizations that have put well-thought-out strategies in place have seen benefits. In a recent *Business Insider* article, a new report released by Capgemini Worldwide based on years of joint research with the MIT Center for Digital Business found that digitally mature companies are, on average, 26 percent more profitable, have a 12 percent higher market capitalization, and get 9 percent more revenue from current assets. The advantage is there in every industry.

There's ample evidence that organizations that proactively embrace social business benefit from the experience. But if you think of it as a threat to be defended against, you will be doomed from the beginning and won't realize the upside.

To safeguard your organization against the misuse of social media, build your marketing organization from the ground up by:

- Creating a climate of inclusion and empowerment.
- Hiring individuals who are active in at least one social network—more than just having a LinkedIn presence. I would seek out people who understand how social networks work—enthusiasts—who know more than the fundamentals.
- Onboarding forward-thinking people who seek out new collaboration platforms, tools, and capabilities.
- Staffing it with people who are naturally inquisitive and resilient and who regard feedback—of any kind—as an opportunity, and not a threat.
- Building competency in data/web analytics and analysis because understanding online activity is key to making intelligent decisions, determining root cause for what's working and what isn't, and enabling your organization to make midcourse corrections to programs.
- Recognizing that at least one person should have a professional journalism background, since publishing is such a key part of the marketing equation; former journalists understand how to communicate with clarity.
- Making it a goal to educate a large number of people within the organization to realize the benefits and to use social channels to spread the word. The goal shouldn't be to media-train a few executives and ghostwrite on their behalf, but to media-train the entire company.

- Seeking out at least one person with a background in direct marketing, since customer segmentation and message targeting are so critical.

Leslie Reiser is an industry-recognized social media, content, and digital marketing authority and speaker, and currently leads IBM's digital strategy, design and development, and program delivery for midsized business across multiple channels. Her global team has reinvented the way IBM uses content to drive opportunity and sales as well as the delivery of integrated solutions to the global marketplace. As a founding member of the ibm.com social web marketing team, Reiser developed both the award-winning social marketing community infoboom. com and MidsizeInsider.com, an IT news site peppered with expert writers that addresses business challenges facing business and technical professionals.

Rikard Steiber
Global Director of Mobile and
Social Ads, Google

Rikard Steiber

There are many metaphors out there for other things in the world that resemble social in some way, and sometimes it's the most unusual that end up producing the best insights. I think about the Slow Food movement that started in Europe about 25 years ago, which has since turned "slow" into a buzzword for any field that indicates painstaking attention to detail, a deep respect for and knowledge of the "ingredients," and a commitment to creating something that lasts. It's not really about moving slowly. It's about not seeking instant gratification.

As marketers, maybe we should think about "slow social." We've seen a handful of high-profile examples in which a brand jumped into social as quickly as it possibly could—setting up campaigns designed to build as large an audience as possible without thinking much about lasting strategy and success. Then the brands deemed social a failure because it wasn't creating conversions. But their problem is that collecting +1s, likes, and followers is "fast social." It's eye-catching and it's gratifying. Marketers would do well to avoid this tempting trap and instead craft a strategy of "slow social," where they pay close attention to the intricate ways in which social fits into the rest of the marketing order, and set up carefully thought-out strategies that allow social to not just cultivate and flourish within their organizations, but create real, lasting impacts on conversions and sales.

Social is part of your digital future. In search queries for top brands, 70 percent of the content that comes up in results is created by users, not by the brands themselves. Being part of the conversation is a must for brands, because choosing not to prioritize social marketing won't make those users stop talking about your brand online. A strategy of "slow social" will mean you spend less time figuring out how to collect +1s and instead create ways that social can make your display, search, television, and even offline advertising even better.

The great news here is that an effective "slow social" strategy is not just for the bleeding edge of early adopter brands. In fact, the brands that may have initially been hesitant to dive into social will be able to commit to it with a firm and detailed plan for success. They'll be able to learn from others' experiences. They'll be addressing social not as a fad that needs to be pounced upon immediately, but as a long-term way of utilizing digital media to incorporate real and authentic human interactions into their marketing, rooted in an ongoing and consistent brand story, rather than campaigns designed to accumulate fans and followers at a breakneck pace. In short, "it's not too late to be early."

Your first step in "slow social"—in setting social up to enhance your brand, performance, and loyalty objectives—is to ensure that it's something your organization can support in the long run. Keeping social sequestered in a corner of the customer service department won't help this; instead, you'll want to create a broad strategy to incorporate social into your whole company so that it, in turn, can easily be incorporated into all your marketing.

The anchor of this can be an executive whom we call the "social champion." This is an employee senior enough to influence decisions across the entire business who has committed to social on both a personal and professional level, and who also uses it actively, whether personally or publicly (or both). He or she needs to be skilled at bringing together people with very different backgrounds and roles, because your next step as a business is to charge the social champion with spearheading a "task force" to address social across the company as a consistent, unified brand.

Organization and structure have been perhaps the most crucial pieces of the equation that became the Slow Food movement—the system of producers, restaurants, and buyers who make it possible for high-quality food to make it from farm to plate. The same goes for any process that emphasizes quality and thoughtful attention to detail, including a social marketing strategy that works. With a social champion in place and a plan for figuring out how social can stretch across your entire business structure, you'll be set up for learning, for dialogue, and soon, for great brand successes. Being social is a core human behavior, but it's a complicated one, and you need the right structure in place at your business to create those magic moments when great experiences can reach the people for whom they are meaningful.

It's not too different from connecting people with great food.

Rikard Steiber is a passionate Internet geek and entrepreneur who manages the global marketing team for mobile and social advertising at Google headquarters in California. Before this, he was the European marketing director for all Google products out of London. In his previous career, he founded and managed Digiscope/XLENT Consulting Groups, cofounded Scandinavia Online in Sweden where he was running the portal business, started a multimedia department at Telia, and worked with brand management at P&G. He holds a master of science degree from SDA Bocconi School of Management, Milan, Italy, and a bachelor of science from Chalmers University of Technology, Gothenburg, Sweden.

Reggie Bradford
Senior Vice President of Product Development, Oracle
Former Founder and Chief Executive Officer, Vitrue

Reggie Bradford

Social at the Center

There's little point in trying to argue that marketing hasn't changed dramatically. And not only has it changed dramatically, but it's done so in a strikingly short period of time, and social has been the key driver for that internal disruption.

Frankly, there would be a lot of advantages to entering brand marketing as a newcomer today as opposed to being deeply ingrained in a legacy marketing organizational structure. Asking a reputable enterprise with long-established tools and processes to not only face the realities of this disruption without hesitation, but to also embrace it and alter the organization to capitalize on it, is a tall order.

At the recent Oracle Social Summit in Las Vegas, David Kirkpatrick, author of *The Facebook Effect* and founder of the Techonomy Conference, told the gathering that the social enterprise is inevitable. And while those at the top of the management pyramid may stress over how social technology is disrupting their hierarchies, this new world of connected, empowered consumers will alter corporate structures just as it's been able to alter entrenched political structures around the globe. He added that it's not unreasonable for employees to wonder if their CEO is the next Hosni Mubarak.

Given the mandate for organizational change, particularly in marketing, here is how I would approach building a marketing organization today from the ground up.

I would make social the fulcrum of my communications strategy

Social is how the modern consumer has grown accustomed to communicating. The social platforms are where they turn for discovery, research, peer-to-peer recommendation (a force far stronger than other influencers like advertising), and for follow-up customer service.

I would use paid and other media to buttress the core social strategy

Paid offers a way to amplify qualified, relevant content that is desired and welcomed with open arms by the consumer. Paid media strategies would be informed by what we learn about the brand's audience through our consistent interaction with them on social, thereby maximizing the effect of every spend.

I would leverage owned channels first, then earned, then paid, followed by events and PR

As the foundation of my marketing strategy, I would put whatever financial and personnel resources were necessary toward fielding and operating world-class Facebook pages, Twitter feeds, Pinterest boards . . . whatever platforms are most appropriate for the brand. Remember, consumer engagement is the top prize, and with the user's ability to either interact with your content or scroll right past it in their news feeds, meaningful content is more critical than ever. Without it, you'll never even get in the batter's box. That content performs on the brand's owned channels and then hopefully elicits earned benefits. Paid media amplifies and capitalizes on content that is performing well. Events and PR are more traditional marketing vehicles, but so are brand touch points that can be consistent with the brand voice established on social, and again, be informed by user data and successes on the social fulcrum.

Yes, in countless marketing departments, social is the enemy of "but this is the way we've always done it." Comfort zones are being challenged. But the ability to pivot and stay in sync with the way today's consumers want to interact and conduct business will be a significant determining factor in which enterprises survive and thrive.

Veteran technology and management executive Reggie Bradford is senior vice president of product development for Oracle, where he brings more than 20 years of experience across technology, Internet, and marketing sectors. Prior to joining Oracle, he was founder and CEO of Vitrue (now a wholly owned subsidiary of Oracle), where he developed the company into the leading provider of social marketing publishing software for global brands and agencies. During his tenure at Vitrue, he led a team that worked with many of the world's premier global brands as well as more than 75 agencies worldwide. Among his many industry accolades and awards, Reggie was named one of Television Week's *"10 to Watch" for 2005, and one of the "Top 10 Entrepreneurs of the Year in 2010" by* Business to Business. *He serves on numerous advisory and nonprofit boards, including BrightWhistle, SoloHealth, and The Brandery.*

Sharon Feder
Chief Operating Officer, Mashable

Looking to a Digital Media Company to Help Build the Next Modern Marketing Agency

Sharon Feder

Brands seek to create exciting campaigns that extend into consumers' lives, both online and off, which creates a new set of demands for marketing agencies. The agencies that succeed will be the ones structured to integrate social and digital from the start, and will be focused on offering creative services that better enable brands to tell stories across their channels in real time. In other words, agencies need to be set up for content creation and distribution. To succeed in this landscape, marketing pros can take a note from modern media companies.

Digital media companies like Mashable are on a mission to provide our readers with a steady stream of compelling content on our site and the social networks they live on. This is largely driven by our newsroom, which creates both timely and evergreen content.

Our newsroom is staffed by journalists who understand how to write content for our community and know what is valuable to them. They also understand how to write titles for social distribution and pick images that are immensely sharable. For the growing number of projects that require multimedia, we have hired staffers with expertise in photo and video. Having an in-house team that can create valuable, sharable assets that speak to our community is a must.

But solid content isn't enough; you need a dedicated team to take these efforts a step further and strategically distribute the content. Our community team constantly evaluates each of our social channels to understand what works and what doesn't. For example, knowing that sharing great images with our stories on Facebook leads to greater engagement, they'll take the time to pick or create strong visuals to share with the right stories. They work with our editors to decide which stories get shared with which network and how they'll be shared. In addition, they create community programs tailored specifically to sites like Pinterest, Instagram, and more.

Our community team is staffed by professionals who started their careers in journalism. They have strong writing backgrounds and communication skills, but are also very research and data driven, which helps us to continually improve our understanding of the Mashable community. They're constantly strategizing new ways to boost engagement among readers.

Another important team that regularly reinvents the way we connect with our community is our product team. We've spent the past year hiring product experts and engineers who have worked collaboratively across the company to reimagine and relaunch Mashable. This is a team that's tapped into industry trends, has a strong feedback loop with our editorial and community teams, and is focused on providing our community with new, innovative experiences.

The entire Mashable site has been built in-house, from the ground up. The process has been a liberating one; it helps to drive innovation within the company, and it frees us from the confines of third-party software. Mashable's chief technology officer, Robyn Peterson, believes it's critical for media companies to innovate and build technology in-house because media companies too often become reliant on third-party services, and then they become service organizations that are focused on implementing other companies' ideas, which aren't necessarily new, original, or competitive.

"We live to create unique products, and we do it with our own two hands," said Peterson. "We build them, and then we integrate them throughout the entire platform and build a consistent experience and strategy."

For example, our product team recently launched Mashable Velocity, a new tool that measures the virality of content on Mashable and predicts which content is about to go viral through a proprietary algorithm. Velocity determines which stories are highlighted on our home page and featured throughout the site. The tech team worked with our editorial and community teams to build out and finesse the product based on their needs. Agencies could really benefit by building in-house tech teams and developing new, innovative products in such a holistic way, integrating feedback from all departments.

At Mashable, we believe that technology and content will power our future, and we think brands and agencies should be thinking the same way. Throughout the day, users move from one device to the next, and your content must seamlessly follow suit. Solid content and a great user experience are critical to building relationships with consumers, and the agencies that are staffed to build creative new solutions will win them over.

As Chief Operating Officer of Mashable, the leading news site for the connected generation, Sharon Feder oversees all business operations. Since joining Mashable, she has significantly grown the editorial team, extended partnerships with leading news publishers, and created a human resources and recruiting function. During her tenure as publisher, the company experienced its fastest growth to date and built its own ad sales operations. She's held the positions of managing editor and features editor at Mashable, and is responsible for building Mashable's native advertising offering. She currently serves on the Social Media Advertising Consortium board and the #GivingTuesday board.

Mike Edelhart
President of the Pivot Conference and Social Week in New York

Mike Edelhart

The question on the table is what kind of marketing organization would I create today from scratch. In truth, however, that may be the wrong question. The very way the question is phrased derives from a traditional view about the future of organization-consumer interaction.

After all, marketing as we have known it in recent history is a response to the fundamental truth that audiences have stood at extreme remove from the sources of content used to attract them. Since the audience was way out . . . there . . . and the media to capture them was created by a small, cloistered set of experts way over . . . here . . . the only way to cross that chasm was through artillery salvos of messaging aimed at targeted sets of those distant consumers. Thus, channels and demographically driven marketing, magazine circulation, Nielsen numbers, and TV campaigns are all artifacts of that reality.

But, today's world has been transformed by the emergence of a new social construct. The social construct is nothing less than a change in how people have chosen to live. Humans, in this generation, have discovered the first ever opportunity, via social, to interact with technology in a purely human fashion. Social allows people to do what they have always done, but in an expanded and intensified manner. And people worldwide have willingly altered the way they live to take advantage of this opportunity: how they buy, date, learn, celebrate, mourn, tell tall tales, build influence, and choose leaders. The construct that results from worldwide response to social online is fundamental and unstoppable, and so has profound implications across society and business.

With social now at the heart of how people do everything businesses care about, the question today shouldn't be, "How would I build a marketing department?" It should be, "How can my organization most effectively understand, reach, and influence the individuals engaged in living this new way?"

Because humans have willingly, gleefully taken their lives onto the worldwide network, essentially every action by every consumer on earth is now available to any organization that wants to look for it. This means that every consumer—and in fact every aspect of every consumer—is directly addressable by organizations.

As a result, the whole idea of lobbing clumps of common messages long distances to reach large, vaguely similar, groups becomes outmoded—inelegant, gross, wasteful, and slow-moving. Marketing, in the traditional sense, and everything that goes with it, now stands on the wrong side of history.

What we can now do, for the first time ever, is directly address any individual at any time in any circumstance with precisely the information, experience, connection, comfort, or bit of engineered serendipity most likely to produce our desired outcome. This process is not, as marketing has been, delineated by demographics; it is a function of analytics.

So, my successor to a traditional marketing department would be centered purely on data. It would aim to capture all data about all the universes of individuals our organization cared about. It would have as its core competencies data visualization and algorithmic structuring of asynchronous human behavior into actionable sets. It would be focused on flexibility, feedback, and full transparency. It would celebrate learning and input as much as messaging and output. Operationally, it would function much more like a hedge fund than an ad agency, with real-time use of information for immediate market advantage, magnified over millions of transactions, in this case, human interactions.

It would also, as a necessity, have deep and direct ties with every part of the organization. When the mechanism for interaction with people in the market shifts this dramatically, other functions inside the organization perforce must change with it. This deep shift in "marketing" compels radical transformation in product development, customer service, and supply chain management. It will, over time, not just completely reshape the face of marketing, but the contour of the corporation as a whole.

Mike Edelhart is an experienced media and Internet start-up executive. A former managing director and founder of First30 Services, a launch accelerator for early-stage companies, Edelhart has held CEO and executive management positions at a range of start-ups and tech companies. Earlier in this career, at SoftBank, he directed content for the Seybold, Interop, and Comdex conferences, and launched new businesses. He has also worked as an Internet strategies consultant to Bloomberg, Reuters, and other major media and Internet companies, and as an advisor to Mass Relevance, Aggregate Knowledge, and SmaSh Technology.

Karen Spiegel
Senior Vice President, Managing Director of Marketing and Communications, R/GA

The motto over the door would be: experiment, improve, repeat.

Karen Spiegel

Top-Down Vision, Bottom-Up Engagement

Settle on a strong, singular point of view that permeates the mission statement, messaging, and culture. Know what business you are in—not just the value you offer your consumer, but also the values you stand for as a brand. Both value and values are demonstrated in what you do as a business and how you do it. Get it right, and you will need less marketing.

Today's marketing teams need to be embedded and possibly decentralized across the company. They need to be agile and able to adjust both strategically and frequently, morphing and iterating with market change. One way to do so is to consider building an ecosystem, where each subsequent product or service introduction enhances the previous one(s). What is your company's value system, and how can you quickly build on it?

That means rethinking what marketing actually is. It's not what's now or what's been; it's what's next! With such a focus, marketing becomes the discipline of uncovering opportunities and building upon core values that are already there with an emphasis on mobile and social. This thinking can be difficult for marketers, even on a small scale, but it can lead to enormous change and a big upside.

Remember the obvious and embrace what you have. At the best companies, employees have always been great brand advocates. But today with social media, their value is of even greater importance. Finding ways to harness their collective voice to support a company's owned and earned media efforts goes a long way to promote the brand with key constituents.

Connected, Connected, Connected

Marketing today is increasingly complex with technological changes and the introduction of new channels. First and foremost, it's essential to create collaboration and cross-functional teams across the company with fewer silos to harness the company's intellectual capital. There is a real need for cohesion across the organization to encourage iteration and prototypes that are created quickly, say within days or one month.

This requires not just the marketing team, but also other disciplines. For instance, marketers should have marketing technology expertise. CMOs, product development, sales, and the CIO need to work together, since business innovation and sales growth require expertise and collaboration from all departments.

Accountable and Responsive to Data

The adage goes: "You get what you measure." Just think about the proliferation of data. With the rising relevance of CRM and behavioral targeting, both tracking complex data sets and analyzing them have become a daunting task. Simultaneously, there is an erosion of accountability due to lack of expertise, oversight, and/or funding—a trend that needs to be reversed for future marketing success.

Marketing departments need to be less reliant on soft, intermediate measures and more accountable to real-time business data. Such responsiveness would go a long way toward the necessary fast turnaround essential in today's environment. Marketing must establish objective measurement benchmarks, where new ideas can be assessed against them. Marketers must become experts in evaluating data, visualizing patterns, and recognizing how to optimize it, by constantly monitoring and changing variables to find causality to increased sales and business results.

So What about Media?

Now more than ever, media needs to be a part of the strategic process and overall planning. The big question for marketers is not what media to buy but rather what, other than your product, could you create that would be invaluable to your audience and keep them coming back. Be less focused on how to stand out in a cluttered media environment and more concerned about how the brand "fits in" to your customers' lifestyle and existing behaviors.

After all, changing behavior is no easy task. So make it simple. Create value for consumers. Encourage internal collaboration and prototyping by developing smaller, more nimble multidisciplinary teams. Galvanize employee participation in owned media. Be your own best advocate. The benefits are huge, the challenges immense. But with no playbook, you can set the rules. And how many times has this been the case?

A 15-year veteran in the digital space, Karen Spiegel directs the global communications strategy for R/GA, partnering with leading brands to broaden the exposure and innovation of their client work. She has positioned the agency as a thought leader in interactive marketing, bringing widespread acclaim to the company and its expanding international footprint in Europe, Latin America, and Asia. Since joining R/GA in 2001, Spiegel's passion for pushing boundaries and building reputations has garnered numerous accolades and awards for the agency, along with notable international conference keynotes and participation in leading analyst reports. She speaks at industry events, including, most recently, DLD Women.

Karen Robinovitz
Cofounder and Chief Creative Officer,
Digital Brand Architects

Karen Robinovitz

Marketing a brand and communicating its missives today is vastly different than it was 10, even 5 years ago. In the past, marketers largely relied on traditional media and public relations, targeting both television and print first and foremost. The idea of anything online was an after-thought, if that.

Today, the roles would be reversed. Most of the budget, time, and energy would be spent on what happens in the digital landscape. It is where people live now—online. It is how we consume knowledge and content, from 60-somethings swiping through the pages of an iPad on the chaise lounge or a young teen, locking herself in her bedroom to read the blogs on multiple gadgets at once while watching TV and texting her friends.

But before anyone runs and out and starts thinking all things social media, the key is to understand a brand's audience online, how they absorb information, the gadgets they rely on, the sites they frequent, where they post their own content, how they tag brands they love, if they tag brands they use. The research is key. There can be no pervasive, impactful strategy without a larger understanding of the space and a brand's positioning in that space.

So take a deep dive. There are plenty of listening tools that will tell you where your audience lives online—are they more Instagram and Pinterest than Facebook and Twitter? Do they watch videos on YouTube for three hours each day or not at all? Which blogs and sites influence them? Do they shop on their phones? Who do they follow online? These are the kinds of questions everyone should know before going into a communications plan.

When it comes to strategy, this is where the traditional brains kick in. Those who are truly native to social may not be adept at overarching brand strategies, and it is this careful balance of old and new schools of thought that, when combined, can innovate and drive the masses to not only respond, but take part in the brand and become marketers by doing so.

A smart and contemporary marketing organization thinks holistically—how does social blend with traditional messages and advertising, and then how do they all go hand in hand with search and every cornerstone of a brand's communications? In the old-guard days, marketing, PR, advertising, they were all in a vacuum, working separately. In today's world, they need to come together, combine forces and let go of the "this is mine and that is yours" territorialism and ask each other, "How do we do this in partnership, toward one common goal?"

There is a lot of noise out there, and it is vital for marketing teams to cut through the clutter, to find a way to grab the attention of a targeted crowd. And while there is an amount of broadcast in that the brand is producing and sharing content and messaging, there must be an equal amount of dialogue, as the world of communications is no longer a one-way conversation but a two-way street.

A degree of fear will always be there, but those who choose not to push through the fear are the ones who will lag. Today's world is impatient and fickle. People move fast and are quick to click off a brand's page or content if they are not either entertained or heard. It is particularly difficult for luxury brands that have always prided themselves on exclusivity. There is a way to be lux and social at once, however, and the trick is finding the right talent who will toe the line and adhere to the brand's DNA while still exploring new ways to reach consumers and enable them to respond publicly.

There is no secret to forming a strong organization in today's day and age as social media is not one size fits all. Like all successful groups, the trick is in the talent, finding the right team of people who think differently, embrace what's new, and respect the tradition of strategy and brand building, then mixing them all together for the most delicious byte.

Karen Robinovitz is responsible for the creative direction of Digital Brand Architects' two divisions: Social Media Strategy and Online Talent Management. The talent management division, dedicated to representing top-tier online content creators, was the first of its kind and has been featured in the New York Times, Women's Wear Daily, Ad Age, *and more. She got her start as a journalist at* Women's Wear Daily *and has contributed to* Marie Claire, Elle, Harper's Bazaar, New York Magazine, *and the* New York Times. *Robinovitz has been featured as a trend expert on several networks and morning shows across the country. She is the coauthor of three books and has spent many years working closely with luxury lifestyle brands, overseeing marketing and targeted partnerships and specializing in digital and social media.*

Stephanie Agresta
Global Director of Social Media and
Digital, MSLGROUP

Stephanie Agresta

For communications agencies, it is critical that we redesign ourselves to address the seismic shifts in marketing created by social media. Building the next generation of agencies requires a diversification of our talent and greater efforts at integrating skill sets. It is no longer possible to just look at the world through a narrow lens or discipline. Specifically in public relations, how we tell stories and how we define influence has fundamentally changed. All of this means that we have to do things very differently moving forward. The next generation of PR firms will:

- **Organize around engaging content and community expertise:** We can no longer focus primarily on traditional media to tell stories through traditional media outlets. Even tacking on social amplification efforts (or blogger relations) is not enough. The process must start with developing engaging multichannel content (for example, content that is newsworthy, entertaining, or useful) and then understanding the communities that share and talk about that content. There is a new set of social media influencers who are defining your brand in very vocal and visible ways. Relationships with those groups and individuals can matter as much as the *New York Times* and the *Wall Street Journal*. The secret sauce is in understanding the intricacies of how these various influential voices reach the digital consumer.
- **Hire new types of talent:** In addition to superior writers and strategic thinkers, the next-generation PR agency must also have internal expertise in video and visual arts, paid content distribution, data and analytics, and mobile application development. Hiring and retaining this talent will be one of the biggest hurdles for any agency striving to be social by design. It is a fiercely competitive marketplace, and agency cultures take time to adapt. Environments that celebrate and foster collaboration will win.
- **Create roles for integrators:** Organizing client work around integrated thinking of multiple skill sets is what will deliver award-winning work in the future. I predict a growing number of "integrator" roles in the agency world. These individuals will build bridges internally and externally to take advantage of the disruption going on inside all marketing organizations.
- **Dig into the data:** The customer life cycle is now more like an infinite loop than a funnel. It is vital that all marketing organizations get much closer to the customer behavior data. How we tackle this

monumental challenge will define success in the years to come. Communications agencies have traditionally been removed from a deep understanding of the customer sales cycle. With greater insight into back-end information, agencies will be able to provide even better community managements services and be able to show real ROI on social media services.

- **Be bold:** Partner with your clients to set testing budgets and new ways of organizing that push the boundaries of how you traditionally operate. Today's system is designed around budget silos, but social media is leading many to break out of that mold. Work closely with your clients to structure approaches that will drive success that can be celebrated internally to drive further change.

As we lead our clients through their own social media journey, next-generation agencies need to look inward and ask challenging questions about the way we are organized and operate.

As MSLGROUP's Global Director of Social Media and Digital, Stephanie Agresta works in partnership with leaders around the global network on social and digital vision, strategy, and talent in support of the agency's global social media offering, Social Hive. In addition to launching "Bloggers Lounge," a networking hub for digital media influencers at the SXSW conference, she founded Stephanie Agresta Consulting, a digital marketing firm that forged partnerships with noted digital thought leaders and emerging technology companies. Stephanie is a popular speaker at industry events, and serves on the board of directors of the Social Media Advertising Consortium. In 2010, she was named to PRWeek's "40 Under 40" roster, and in the same year, her first book, Perspectives on Social Media Marketing, *was released.*

Ian Schafer
Chief Executive Officer and Founder,
Deep Focus

Institutions will try to preserve the problem to which they are the solution.
—Clay Shirky

Ian Schafer

I probably invoke that quote once a day, to remind others and myself that, in case you missed it, we are in a constant state of disruption. If you don't adapt, you will be disrupted. If you don't disrupt yourself, someone will do it for you.

If I were to build a marketing organization from scratch today, it would have two characteristics: integrated and self-disruptive.

I'd begin with the notion that by nature, marketing organizations, be they brands or agencies, are all behind. And they always will be. The ones that are closest to the consumer will be the ones that are best prepared. Advertising doesn't set trends much anymore, anyway—it capitalizes upon them. Brands are less likely to define what is relevant than ever before. Thanks to the empowerment that social media has given every consumer, "relevance" now lies in *their* hands. The marketing organizations that will thrive are the ones that will be able to adapt to the fickleness of and be closest to consumers, while enabling their brands to act faster and smarter by making informed decisions that can manifest in real time—not in traditional creative or campaign cycles. The marketing organizations of today are generally not close enough to overcoming attribution or even measurement challenges to feel informed enough or comfortable. Everything is a moving target, and everything is in perpetual motion.

As time goes on, every marketing organization will need to be in a constant state of flux, and will have to get very good at disrupting themselves. The only way to be well positioned for the future is to accept that it is uncertain—which means structuring as a self-disruptive organization. Budget and time would be set aside to regularly encourage self-disruption.

The always-on, ever-changing nature of social media has made traditional market research and segmentation seem slow and outdated by comparison. This new marketing organization would also be in perpetual motion.

I rather like Newton's first law of motion to capture the essence of it all: "An object at rest stays at rest, and an object in motion stays in motion with the same speed and in the same direction unless acted upon by an unbalanced force." If we're not our own unbalanced force, another one will find us.

The marketing organization of the future is one that moves at the speed of the consumer *and* of culture.

Named a "Media Maven" by Advertising Age *and one of* Adweek's *"Young Ones," Ian Schafer, CEO and founder of Emmy Award–winning, integrated digital agency Deep Focus, is one of advertising's most influential voices in interactive marketing and social media. Deep Focus is powered by social media and has been lauded for its excellence in using digital media, technology, creative, and communications strategies to create engaging, value-driven experiences that get people talking. Schafer also sits on the executive board of the Social Media Advertising Consortium and the Global Advisory Board of Global Social Media Week.*

Joe Burton
President and Chief Operating Officer,
SocialChorus

Joe Burton

I run a social media start-up. I was tempted to answer with the typical social-is-everything rant.

"Social at the center. Think real-time newsroom. Listening, responding, creating content on demand. A social epicenter that understands relationships and the precise content to deliver at the precise moment to drive deeper insights, increasing sales and the knowledge of how to rinse and repeat with better results. All investments flow from this center."

Throw in a few overused buzzwords (authenticity, influence, geo-targeting, etc.) and . . . magic!

But integrated marketing is more complicated than that. And the real answer isn't as clever: focus on good architecture.

Great CMOs are like great architects: they both worry about foundation, environment, design and managing budgets, and a diverse set of discipline experts to create something of lasting quality. Accordingly, I'm stealing ideas (another trait shared by CMOs and architects) from Frank Lloyd Wright:

"Form follows function—that has been misunderstood. Form and function should be one, joined in a spiritual union."

Create a connected, global organization. CEO and CMO in lock-step. Sales and marketing actually working together. Embrace technology, eliminate redundancy, maximize utility, and plan for scalability.

The CMO's organization should be a highly experienced team of cross-disciplined experts driving the process. Fewer administrators. More implementers. You will always need discipline experts to drive their craft (creative, media, PR, etc.); some silos can't be avoided. Electricians can't do the plumbing. Constant collaboration is key. It's also important to determine which investments can be centralized to serve the organization across the spectrum of marketing (data and analytics, production, tech platforms, etc.). Create best-in-class capabilities; otherwise everyone builds everything.

It's easy for a global marketing organization to grow out of control. It just happens. Country by country, product by product, budget by budget. CMOs come and go. The result can be less global marketing organization and more a loose collection of tactical, semiaffiliated budget holders.

"Simplicity and repose are the qualities that measure the true value of any work of art."

Build for greatest impact, and keep it simple. An architect usually determines the best views and designs around the environment to maximize that experience. Successful CMOs need a central focus to drive revenue.

Manage your marketing budget as one investment pool (internal staff and external agency fees, production, media, etc.) to drive success. That pool should be fluid, with investments allocated around intended impact, not discipline. This will result in much smaller internal teams (fewer levels, less juniors), more "on-demand" partnerships, and significantly more working media investments.

"I never design a building before I've seen the site and met the people who will be using it."

Know your team. Place authority and responsibility within the organization in the hands of the people and disciplines that understand your focus and can best drive the organization forward. The doorman can't manage the building. Today, authority is usually in the hands of those with the largest budgets. But what if those budgets developed organically over decades of internal politics? For example, in an expanding number of cases, media folks have inherited power because media budgets are big. If your media team/agency is brilliant and can truly work across all channels with deep consumer insights, that can be good. If not (and it's a rare case indeed), that can be bad.

Likewise, procurement should be working *for* the CMO to help drive better, more efficient (internal and external) relationships, not just cheaper marketing. Tremendous waste goes unchecked inside of many global advertisers, while every external penny is audited, confirmed, and negotiated within an inch of its life.

"Reduce the whole of its parts into the simplest terms, getting back to first principles."

With the proliferation of new digital and social channels, CMOs are faced with two approaches: "We need more people to focus on an increasing number of tactics," or "We can use technology to drive scale, insight, and accountability with fewer people."

The modern CMO has to select and manage an expanding number of best-in-class partners across a wide array of channels. Once you select great partners, trust them to deliver their craft. This includes trusting them to optimize and drive performance. Set guidelines and manage to success. Don't manage tactics, don't audit deliverables, and don't filter partners through a gauntlet of junior marketers. Set the bar high, let them perform, and hold them accountable.

Service providers will mirror your structure. They will embrace your efficiency or your dysfunction. Your actions determine the quality and cost of those relationships.

If you design an organization that is easy to service, it will be lean, fast, and repeatable. Bloated organizations are slow, wasteful, and costly. Green versus conventional building.

"An architect's most useful tools are an eraser at the drafting board and a wrecking ball at the site."

Integrated marketing requires integrated leadership, dynamic investment, and informed and enabled partners. Drive for revenue, simplicity, and efficiency. Lead with courage and flexibility. And like any great architect, make additions and changes with the total integrated structure in mind.

CMOs who are unhappy with their current organization may find it cheaper to tear down and rebuild. Getting the permits is the tricky part.

Joe Burton has spent his career in strategic operational, production, and financial roles working with Fortune 500 clients in more than 50 countries. Prior to joining SocialChorus, he was an entrepreneur in the social and digital media space and was global chief operating officer of two of the largest advertising agency networks in the world: McCann Worldgroup and Ogilvy One Worldwide. An alumnus of Harvard Business School, he is a thought leader and frequent speaker in the areas of social and digital media, integrated marketing services, production capabilities, client/agency benchmarking, compensation, and negotiations.

Alan Osetek
Global President, Resolution Media,
an Omnicom Media Group Company

Alan Osetek

Many people still liken social media to the Wild West. The rules change quickly—you either keep up or risk getting trampled by your own social media strategies. Unfortunately, this prevents many brands from attempting to create a social media presence. Social marketing is not a new concept. If we think back to the Wild West, people used word-of-mouth marketing whenever they purchased something from the general store and then told a neighbor about it. Or, consider a family who bought a brand new TV in the 1950s and invited friends by the house to check out this new technology. The behavior and desire to share knowledge hasn't changed over the years, but the ability to communicate has evolved.

With the advent of smartphones, tablets, and other new socially oriented technologies, consumers can instantaneously tell not only their close friends, but others in their social circles about purchases, behaviors, and activities.

The harsh reality for those lacking a social marketing strategy is that social media is here to stay, and it continues to become a more integrated part of the digital marketing mix. Even traditional marketing means have evolved to incorporate social. TV shows use Twitter hashtags at the bottom of the screen for promotion. Google adopted social into its search algorithm—not only through Google+, but also by accounting for social signals, as well as aggregating trending topics on their main Search Engine Results Page via news alerts and trending videos and images. Whether it's Facebook, Twitter, Google+, or Pinterest, having a social outlet is vital for consumers. Social has become critical to the digital ecosystem and to everyday culture. One of the most important things marketers can do is create an integrated strategy to incorporate social. Why is integration vital? Social media does not exist in a silo, and consumers don't take a single approach toward consumer media and seeking information. Consumers don't say, "Oh, I'm going to search for X. After that, I'm going to turn on the TV and then maybe I'll go on Twitter." Consumers are empowered—they are looking for an answer, and they will utilize any outlet to get to the answer, including word of mouth, social, mobile, TV, and so on. Empowered consumers focus on results, meaning they are not loyal to one brand and will use the latest technology to get questions answered. Empowered consumers are surrounded with multiple outlets to find answers to questions. So, how do marketers get and stay in front of empowered consumers?

Though the rules of social media change quickly, creating a strategy to incorporate social follows the same principles as adopting any other marketing practice. Marketers must first determine business goals and objectives. The second step is to research and identify which empowered consumers they should target. By determining behavior and devices used, marketers can establish where social fits within the empowered consumer's journey. The success of a social campaign is determined like anything else, with the appropriate metrics and key performance indicators. Resolution Media recently conducted a paid social research study in conjunction with Kenshoo Social. The study discovered new metrics to measure the success of a paid search campaign, including exposure rate (of paid Facebook ads shown, how often brands are reaching their desired target audience) and the importance of frequency (how often any brand's ads are shown to the average Facebook user). Are these the be-all and end-all of social metrics? No. But as empowered consumers evolve, so will technology, social media, and the metrics used to measure success.

Social marketing is not going anywhere. In order to stay relevant to the empowered consumer, marketers need a social strategy. This is not an optional part of the marketing plan. The fast-paced, fluid nature of social media and technology may be daunting, but human behavior remains consistent. Social media gives marketers opportunities that the general store proprietors of the Wild West or the TV salesman of the 1950s never had: an ability to communicate with consumers instantaneously—whenever and wherever.

A digital industry veteran, Alan Osetek oversees the global growth and expansion of Resolution's SEM and Social Practices. He previously served as chief revenue officer for Visual IQ, the world's leading cross-channel marketing intelligence software company. Before that, Osetek held various positions throughout his tenure with the Aegis PLC/Isobar family of companies, including executive vice president of global business development, corporate development, cross-unit integration, and global client services. He was responsible for organically building or acquiring new service offerings for the Aegis/Isobar network, and he spearheaded the acquisition and integration of two digital marketing firms: Molecular and iProspect. Prior to joining Isobar, Osetek was president and founder of the digital marketing agency Vizium, which he sold to Aegis PLC in 2001.

INDEX